D1403451

HDBugbee

Great Roundup

GREAT ROUNDUP

ROUNDUP

The Story of Texas and Southwestern Cowmen

By LEWIS NORDYKE
Author of "Cattle Empire"

CASTLE BOOKS

This edition published in 2001 by Castle Books,
A division of Book Sales Inc.
114 Northfield Avenue, Edison, NJ 08837

Reprinted by arrangement with and permission of
William Morrow, an imprint of HarperCollins Publishers
10 East 53rd Street, New York, New York 10022-5299

Library of Congress Catalogue Card No. 57–5599

ISBN 0-7858-1318-7

FOR

HENRY BELL

Contents

Illustrations

9

Hauling in 1883. Ox team here shown before the uncompleted courthouse at Albany.

Between pages 192 and 193

A herd rounded up at the base of Sawtooth Mountain in the Big Bend Country.

An early dipping-vat scene.

Famous men of the frontier, the range and the trail.

Will Rogers with John Carson and John R. Blocker.

Range rig on the Matador.

In town on Saturday.

The Scotland Yard of the range.

Chief of the rustler chasers—Henry Bell.

Present-day home of the Texas and Southwestern.

Cowmen register for their record-breaking convention in Dallas.

Foreword

> They say there'll be a great roundup,
> Where cowboys, like cattle, will stand
> To be cut by the Riders of Judgment
> Who are posted and know every brand.

This isn't *that* great roundup of cowmen, and there is no judgment here! This is a roundup of the deeds and yarns of those cowmen who live out where horizons reach far before they touch a limitless sky and where yarns and deeds are often in fitting proportions.

This story, like a ranch, has a headquarters—and here the home-place is with the virile, seventy-eight-year-old Texas and Southwestern Cattle Raisers Association, which, through its years, has been made up of men who are a special breed of the West—men like Old Man Day and his boys.

On a bright April morning in 1860, Jesse Day and two of his sons, Bill and Dock, were starting to drive a herd of longhorn cattle across the surging flood waters of the Brazos River at Waco, Texas. The father plunged his horse into the foaming current, hoping that the cattle, now urged by the boys, would follow his lead. He and his horse went under. The sons fished out their dad's body. They took it back to a nearby village and sorrowfully gave it temporary burial. Then they forced the cattle across the swirling river and moved on northward.

They intended to drive to Kansas City. They blazed their own route, for this was several years before the trails were established from Texas to Kansas.

At the Missouri border, the boys were halted by armed farmers who believed Texas cattle to be bedeviled with disease. Thus headed off, the Days wandered with their herd and finally reached St. Louis. There they sold the cattle profitably and bought a bunch of horses which they trailed to Louisiana for sale to sugar plantations.

Soon after their return to the family farm near Austin, Texas, the boys went back up the trail, removed the body of their father and took it home for final rest. Then they started gathering another herd of cattle.

Through the years, the grit and the determination exemplified by the suddenly bereaved Day boys have remained in the basic build of cowmen; there have survived on the range from its frontier start a definite individualism and an independence of spirit. I saw an example of these qualities in action not so long ago.

Early in January of 1953, I attended a meeting of the directors of the Texas and Southwestern in the Longhorn Room of the Texas Hotel in Fort Worth. I discerned a strange tension—like that of the instant between a flash of lightning and a clap of thunder—among the half a hundred men who had come off the ranches from all over Texas.

Jack Roach, a tall, bronzed, soft-spoken rancher from the Panhandle country, was then the president. He introduced assorted topics—cattle rustling, disease control, freight rates, marketing problems. But the stockmen kept shifting their eyes toward a telephone booth.

Presently a young cowman stepped from the booth and high-heeled it to the front of the room. Mr. Roach asked him whether he had any news.

"I have just talked into the room where General Eisenhower is working on his inaugural address and his State-of-the-Union message," the young cowman said. "It seems very definite that he will come out hard and fast against all government controls on beef cattle, and that's what we want." Applause welcomed the news from Washington. Though record-breaking drought and a price slump were upon these cowmen, they stood steadfastly against a government-subsidized beef cattle business.

For years I have wanted to write the story of the *bona fide* range cowmen, which would also be the story of the start of the beef cattle business in Texas and its spread to the rangelands of the West. I found that the men of the Texas and Southwestern, which had its start where the Western cattle industry started, had been more actively in the saddle than any other cowmen; they had interested themselves in the forces that had affected beef raising everywhere.

And so here is that story of the Texas and Southwestern cattlemen—the land, the weather, the relentless change and the politics with which they dealt.

This association has had more than one hundred thousand members, each worth his own story. In the following pages are the names of many. Yet the story of those unmentioned is here as well, for it took all of them—all the daring unnamed as well as those written about—to conquer a wilderness and develop a pastoral pursuit as old as Adam into the complex industry it is today.

LEWIS NORDYKE

Amarillo, Texas,
July 4, 1954.

Great Roundup

· 1 ·

Under the Old Oak Tree

Three bewhiskered horsemen jogged across wide, mesquite-dotted Dillingham Prairie toward the raw little village of Graham on the frontier of northern Texas—not far from the Indian Nations over Red River to the north. They had saddled up and pulled out at dawn that chilly February 15 in 1877. Caught in the bright, slanting rays of the rising sun, as they neared the town, the men cast enormous shadows that moved with a rhythmic steadfastness over the flat, wintry landscape.

These riders were men who had fought many a battle over the years with the severities of the cow-country frontier and accepted the hazards of being among the first to drive herds over the long, challenging trails. This sunrise, they were riding directly into a cattlelands drama of near-epic proportions, and the shadows they cast as early protagonists were not transient, but remain today when the suns of another century brighten the same vast sky.

These were men of action. And the consequences of their actions that day were to affect every cowman living and yet to be born; likewise they would affect every twenty-five-dollar-a-month cowboy, every red-handed rustler for generations. This ride across the frontier prairie would, as roundup followed roundup, continue to the capitals of the range states, to cities like St. Louis and Chicago, to the White

House, the United States Supreme Court and beyond international boundaries. The force they unleashed would, in its own way and in due time, battle in the really big range wars —those between individuals, regions, states and even nations. But the men could not foresee that unending trail; they had only a determined plan to organize frontier cowmen in a unified and unrelenting war on cattle rustlers. They had, by letter, word of mouth and advertisements in the few newspapers, invited all stock growers in sparsely populated northwestern Texas to gather at Graham to consider a means of joining forces. This union of rugged individuals against a common enemy would grow into today's Texas and Southwestern Cattle Raisers Association, which in 1954 had a membership of ten thousand stockmen in all the range states —cowmen who can still tell time by the sun and ride out both good times and bad.

The generations of cowmen who have been banded together in the Texas and Southwestern have never attempted to boss the wide range of the West. Yet they have been natural leaders since their association came into being in a strategic place—Texas, where the Western beef business started with mossy-headed longhorns of Spanish origin—and at the right time—when campfires twinkled along the miles of the Old Chisholm Trail and the great frontier was being rolled all the way back by men on horses and in butcher-knife wagons who had to fight, plan and endure to succeed in conquering this hard land.

U. S. Grant was then President of the United States, just thirteen years united again, and if he had sent to the western-most state of the old Confederacy for representative cattlemen to confer with him about conditions in the Southwest, the three who called the meeting at Graham would have been well qualified to journey eastward. But the President hadn't sent, and the path to Washington with advice was at that particular time an untrodden one. The cattle business had no choice but to be self-reliant. And there were no more self-reliant men anywhere than these.

C. C. Slaughter, tall, affable and gallant, with his groomed beard a little brushier than a goatee, was the first native-born cattle king of Texas and had just turned forty. He had started on his own in the cattle business when he was seventeen years old with $520 he had made by hauling and trading lumber and wheat in the more thickly populated central part of Texas, along the Trinity River. He invested the money in a herd of cattle and in a short time moved them three hundred miles northwest, away from the encroachments of civilization. There he ran the vast Long S Ranch on Dillingham Prairie, where the three men had spent the night. He also had a home in Dallas, for he had recently branched out into the banking business there.

The second rider, Jim Loving, had been born in Kentucky. He had lines in his face and a tired slump to his shoulders that made him look older than his forty-one years. There was gray in the full mustache and the pointed beard. His father before him had been a cowman and a good one, known throughout the West, where he had blazed cattle trails with Col. Charles Goodnight. The father, Oliver Loving, had been killed in a Comanche ambush a few years before at the Horse-head Crossing on the Pecos—out in the rough western country where that storied river slants across the state line from New Mexico into Texas. Jim, following in his father's bootsteps, had been a big cattle operator and trail driver. But the scattered fires in which rustlers heated their brand-changing irons to a sizzling white had been built around his herds until now he was broke. All Loving had left, except his good name, was his little Lost Valley Ranch in Jack County.

C. L. (Kit) Carter of Palo Pinto County was the third horseman. He was fifty-seven years old and wore a Santa Claus beard and mustache. He had an unswerving integrity and a friendly spirit that was reflected in the kindly twinkle in his eyes. Carter's birthplace was Pittsylvania County, Virginia, but he had moved to Texas when he was a young man. Like Jim Loving, he had an Indian-caused sorrow buried deep in a corner of his heart.

The riders were about the same as kinfolks, all being of a genuine breed of bow-legged men that had developed on the cattlelands frontier. They were stock growers. Each had abandoned the comparative safety of the more populous settlements and had ventured to the open spaces where a man could have forty miles of elbow room, though he was sure to have to use elbow grease and guts to hold it. The three were long-time friends; they had been in cattle deals, they had worked roundups in all kinds of weather, and they had survived Indian depredations.

Now a new foe had hit: cattle rustling had become big busi-

ness, ruinous for nearly every stockman in the wide bounds of vulnerable, unfenced northwestern Texas.

At chance meetings for over a year, Slaughter, Loving and Carter had speculated heatedly on ways of battling the rustler. John N. Simpson, whose ranch was in Parker County, had told them at one time of the Wyoming Stock Growers Association, which had been set up to police the roundups and to keep eyes open for suspected thieves. Some of the southern Texas cowmen had likewise formed a small association to protect themselves from border bandits.

Within the past few months, Loving, Carter, Slaughter and Simpson had met oftener and developed the embryo of a plan.

Nearly all the northwest Texas cowmen were fiercely independent, each man taking his own risks, win or lose. However, the rustlers were beginning to run in efficiently operated gangs and the victims had almost reached the point of desperation.

"We'll fight fire with fire! We'll gang up on them!" Slaughter said at one get-together. "We'll help each other. If you, Loving," he continued, "saw cattle bearing Carter's brand in a trail herd or in the possession of strangers, you could—if you had an organization back of you giving you the right—take over the cattle, send a cowboy after Carter and hang onto—or hang up—the cattle thieves."

"Boys—" Carter's kindly eyes were dead serious. "Boys, let's keep down the violence. There's been so much—"

"And we can work out our roundups so we'll be sure no dirty rustlers are rounding up our yearlings," Simpson said. His herds had also been hit hard.

Thus the men had evolved a system by which every stock grower could act as a detective for his neighbor, though that neighbor might live thirty miles away.

Several dogs ran out to bark with early-morning vigor at the horses as Slaughter, Loving and Carter rode down the rutted main street of Graham. Smoke from the chimneys of the small homes, most of them unpainted, lazed upward into the now brilliant blue sky, leaving a fragrant tang in the air. The riders saw a dozen horses, slightly humped and their hair fuzzed up because of the chill in the southwest breeze, tied to trees and to the gallery posts of the Richards House, the one hotel. There were also saddled horses in front of the saloon across the strip of rough earth that was still more of a road than a street.

The morning air was cold enough to turn the hot breath of the horses into vapor, and a team hitched to a rusty old wagon standing in the shade in front of the general store looked as if they were snorting smoke. Graham was little more than a frontier outpost, and its general store, mingling the smells of apples, oranges, onions, side bacon, saddles, dry goods and slick brown coffee beans, was the mecca of all the families living in Young County.

The men tied their horses in a sunny spot and hurried into the lobby of the hotel, where an apple-bellied stove warmed a friendly circle of lounging men. Some of them were joshing Dan Waggoner because of a fast one he had pulled, or was being accused of pulling.

A rustler had rounded up 144 of Waggoner's 3-D steers and neatly burned a box around the brand, making it the Boxed 3-D. After observing the artistic deviltry, Waggoner knew that he couldn't prove the steers had ever been his. He rode into town and searched the brand records in the county clerk's office. Finding no such brand as the Boxed 3-D on the books, he immediately registered the mark in his own name. Out on the range he reclaimed his steers from the surprised brand burner.

Cowmen kept crowding into the little lobby, coming singly, in pairs and in groups. Some of the ranchers had traveled more than one hundred miles and had made overnight stops at ranch homes by the way, where warm hospitality always welcomed the traveler. The new arrivals gathered around the stove, wiping the dampness off their mustaches, blowing their noses and then turning their backs to the fire. Kit Carter, Slaughter and Tom Waggoner glanced at Jim Loving when Charlie Dalton walked in. Loving busied himself at the important task of fingering mud off his boots. There was no outright enmity between Dalton and Loving, but cause enough for embarrassment whenever they met in a crowd acquainted with Loving's troubles. Back in 1870, the Dalton family had sold a herd to Loving for $15,000 on credit. When the rustler-ravaged Loving went broke, Dalton had to reclaim what was left of the cattle to settle his debt.

To create a diversion someone began to chide A. B. Medlan, saying he had turned granger. Rustlers had raided him so constantly that Medlan had sold out nearly all his cattle and had started raising corn, wheat and hay to sell to stockmen. He had been a cowman since 1854 and had managed to stick it out during the Civil War and subsequent Indian raids, but the rustlers had been too much for him.

"Have you joined up with the Farmers Alliance?" John Simpson twitted him.

"No," said Medlan, "the Knights of Labor are my bunch."

Some of the men accused Medlan of getting over on the side of Cain and reminded him that the Lord preferred the offering of Stockman Abel to Granger Cain's.

The Farmers Alliance and the Knights of Labor, which eventually joined hands and hearts, represented the first efforts of farmers and labor to organize in the Southwest—efforts along the same line the cowmen had in mind in Graham that day.

Gradually the joking stopped, and as men remembered the reason for their being there the meeting took on a conspiratorial air. Rather than secrete themselves in a crowded room behind bolted doors, the cowmen preferred as always the outdoors and sought secrecy so far out in the open that no intruder could hear. They filed out of the hotel and headed toward a nearby tree. It was a huge gnarled oak, which was then about two hundred and fifty years old.

One man looked up at the large, reaching branches and observed that such limbs would be mighty handy for stringing up any rustlers that happened to be in the crowd. Another acknowledged that just a few years before he had seen some horse thieves hanging from those very branches. "But there's not enough trees in the country to hang all the derned cow thieves on now—even if we could catch them dirty son-of-a-guns," he said.

The men gathered in a circle about the size and shape of the oak's winter shade. Some of them stood; others squatted on their heels. Here were forty honest men gathered together to plot against the thieves. They weren't dashing, flashily sombreroed cowboys; rather, they were bewhiskered, coarsely clad ranchers. A few of the younger men represented the new slick-faced generation. Burk Burnett had a neat little mustache that he could reach with an upward thrust of his lower lip, but he had no beard or sideburns. A few of the men sported short, muttonchop beards.

These were the first cowmen of Texas and the Southwest; they had started the business and spread it across a wide strip of country from Texas to Canada, and into Canada. They were called Texans, but actually they weren't, except by choice. C. C. Slaughter was probably the only native Texan in the group. The men had migrated to the fabled land of Texas mainly from the older Southern states. The migration had begun, as in the case of the Slaughters, even before the Texas Revolution and had accelerated after the Civil War. Men in the defeated South had looked for new terrain, and Texas, with its growing cattle industry, its space and freedom, became for them a land of new beginnings.

All the men gathered under the tree at Graham responded to the urge to get out on the wide, untrammeled land as far as possible from the settlements, out on the far fringe of the frontier where men lived by the code of the range. According to this code a man was as good as his word. The man who reneged or double-crossed or lied his way out was a thief and a scoundrel and actually considered worse than a killer—if the killer was within his rights as they were interpreted on the frontier.

Justice was hard and not burdened with technicalities. The main interpretation of the code was that a man couldn't be morally innocent and legally guilty; if he shot another, did he have a right to do it? This was brought out clearly by one judge in whose court a prisoner was brought to face a charge of murder. The judge soberly asked, "Was there a grudge between them? Was it a fair fight?"

And a few years before the gathering of cowmen at Graham, George Reynolds found that a man could get into sustained trouble with the law by not killing a horse thief.

Reynolds and his future father-in-law, J. B. Matthews, had been hunting cattle in Palo Pinto County. With them, working as cowboy-horse wrangler, was a man called Jacko, a youngster Reynolds had befriended several times. One bitterly cold day Reynolds left Jacko in charge of the camp.

When Reynolds, Matthews and their men returned, they couldn't find Jacko, but they soon "cut his sign." Jacko had departed on Reynolds' favorite horse; moreover, he had taken all the blankets, leaving the men with the unpleasant prospect of sleeping in the cold without cover.

Reynolds and Si Hough picked up Jacko's trail and followed it. Along the way, another cowman, Tom Crammer, joined them.

Some thirty miles away they found Jacko at a ranch house, and they recovered all the loot, including a stout rawhide lariat. Reynolds decided to turn Jacko over to the sheriff, and the men and their prisoner started the long trip to the Palo Pinto jailhouse.

A few hours later they met another cowman and told him of their experience with the now cowering Jacko.

"Why bother to take him to jail?" the cowman said, pointing to a large post oak. "Why not just string him up to a limb over there and be done with it?"

This sounded like practical frontier justice on a very cold day. So the men looped the rawhide lariat over Jacko's neck and tossed the other end over a large limb. In keeping with the code of the range, they gave Jacko the privilege of making a final statement or "making peace with your God."

Jacko, with his chin elevated by the rawhide around his neck, prayed. He uttered such a fervent plea for life that Reynolds decided to give him a good whipping and turn him loose.

Reynolds applied the rawhide to Jacko's rear instead of his neck, gave the wretch an overcoat and told him to make tracks.

The first reports of the episode to reach Palo Pinto had it that Jacko had been caught stealing a horse and had been strung up. The sheriff joined the others in saying good riddance. However, when the truth was known, the sheriff was greatly disturbed; he must jail Reynolds! It was a penitentiary offense to give a man a country lashing of the sort Jacko had received.

In order to keep out of jail and run his ranch, Reynolds dodged the not-too-aggressive sheriff for three years, and he didn't go into town until one day a great necessity arose. Reynolds needed a marriage license to wed Lucinda Elizabeth Matthews, a slight, quiet, cultured young lady. Still fearing arrest, he enlisted the aid of Tom Crammer and another friend, and, all armed with shotguns and pistols, they went to town and obtained the marriage license.

Reynolds and his bride set up housekeeping in a one-room, sod-thatched dugout on the ranch, she to join the ranks of the frontier's lonely women—like Mrs. Carter, Mrs. Loving and Slaughter's mother—some of them a day's ride from the nearest neighbor.

The men under the tree had known only this life all their days on the frontier, and now for the first time they had come together with the idea of forming a permanent posse.

John N. Simpson walked to the center of the circle, holding his hat in his hand.

"Gentlemen," he said, "come to order. I've been roped in by Kit Carter to start things off. So we'll consider the meeting has come to order. I move that Kit Carter serve as chairman."

The motion carried, and Carter stepped forward, clearing his throat and pulling on his beard. Jim Loving was named secretary, and he fished from his pockets some old letters to write on, and a pencil.

Then the big talk started. Slaughter, Carter, Loving and Simpson explained their plan briefly, pointedly. W. B. Slaughter, a brother of C. C., jumped up. "I think," he said, "that it is the sense of this group to organize an association of cowmen. It's about the only thing we *can* do under the circumstances. So I make a motion that the chairman appoint a committee to work out the objects and purposes of this meeting and our proposed organization."

Chairman Carter named the committee, selecting men from every part of the vast territory, many of whose names are famous in the beef cattle business—Joe Graham, Sam Gleason, Rowland Johnson, A. B. Medlan, C. B. Brummett, J. T. Webb, George Wright, H. H. Simpson, Jim Loving, R. E. Mabry, H. G. Bedford, Tom Merrill, John D. Smith, W. B. Slaughter, D. B. Gardner, J. C. Lindsey. Chairman Carter joined the committee, which retired to a tiny hotel room to ponder the problems of cowmen whose herds grazed the hills and prairies of the open range. The Southwestern cattle business as we know it today had begun to take shape there in the shade of an old oak tree.

The Kind That Keep Cattle

While members of the committee labored at the arduous task of expressing the purposes and methods of organization in written words properly spiced with "herebys" and "whereases," the other ranchers gathered in the hotel lobby after supper and enjoyed the comforts and companionship offered by the trip to town. They sat, stood and milled around the black stove resting in the middle of the ash-filled box, which made a dandy spittoon. As they talked their conversation painted a background for the work the committeemen were doing in one of the little rooms above them.

Many of the men had never met before, since this territory was so vast, and strangers in a crowd meant new stories and an excuse to retell familiar ones.

In this new and changing land, the laws were still being made. Cowmen working together could exert a powerful influence, although the rules they favored might seem hard or one-sided to latecomers, since they were the men who had conquered the dangers later settlers would only hear about. There had been no droughts in the blood and sweat they had spilled to free the land from fear. A certain strength had been required of them, and they believed that the space that had been paid for so dearly should be a land for men who were fair in their dealings and who were unafraid.

Speaking of men like these, S. D. Barnes, an early-day

editor, said, "It would be ridiculous to claim that all the Texans were formed in heroic mold, for they were only human after all, and possessed their due share of human faults and weaknesses. Still, cowardice was so uncommon as to be thought worthy of special mention."

If these men had been weaklings or cowards they wouldn't have been ranching in northwestern Texas nor meeting in Graham, for this country had been subjected to the fiercest Indian warfare. They would have long ago fled to a safer place; they would have been winnowed out as was a man known to Big Foot Wallace, a noted Indian fighter of the Southwest. In his memoirs, Wallace told of an encounter with a band of Comanches.

"When the Indians were charging us so fiercely," he wrote, "I saw one of my men skulking behind a clump of prickly pears. I went to him and told him to come out and fight like a man.

" 'Cap,' he said, 'I would if I could, but I can't stand it.' I saw by the way his hands shook and his lips quivered that he was speaking the truth. I replied, 'Well, stay there then if you must, and I will say nothing about it.'

"But some of the rest noticed him, and if I had not interposed they would have killed him, and I might just as well let them, for the poor fellow had no peace in his life afterward. . . . But after all, bravery is about as safe from harm as cowardice. This man was the only one wounded, besides one other who was slightly nicked . . . an arrow flew where he was hiding, struck him in the arm and pinned him to the prickly pear behind which he was concealed."

Big Foot Wallace would have felt at home in this group of men with their history of hair-raising experiences, grief and narrow escapes. They had lived so long under the constant strain of expected Indian raids that occasionally one of them walked cautiously to the hotel door to take a look around.

The long siege of depredations had ended with the successful corralling of the red men on their reservations, and there hadn't been a murderous raid within the past two years. But still the men, from long habit, were alert. There was scarcely a man among them who didn't carry scars of wounds from arrows, knives or rifle shots somewhere under his long-handled underwear, if not on his face or scalp.

When George Reynolds eased over to the door to look "at the weather," he carefully braced his back with a hand because of an old arrowhead still lodged there.

It had been embedded in his muscles since April 3, 1867, just short of ten years now.

The story was retold that night of February 15, 1877, in the hotel, with several men adding their bit. Reynolds, his brother, William D., and eight other cowboys got into an Indian fight at the mouth of the Double Mountain Fork of the Brazos, in what is now Haskell County. An arrow hit Reynolds in the stomach and he crumpled off his horse. He yanked the wooden shaft from the wound, but the head of the arrow remained. Si Hough rode up to him and asked, "Which Indian did that?"

"The one with the red shirt," Reynolds said. He was barely able to talk.

"By damn! I'll have that Indian's hair!" Hough said and spurred his horse. In a few minutes he returned to Reynolds with a bleeding scalp and said, "Here's your man with the red shirt."

When the fight was over, six Indians were dead, but no one could figure out a way to remove the arrowhead from Reynolds' back. He was carried home, sixty miles and twenty-four hours away, on the backs of two pack horses. The nearest doctor was still one hundred and ten miles away. When the doctor arrived five days later Reynolds was well on his way to recovery, and it wasn't long until he was back in the saddle.

"When you goin' to have that arrow dug out of your backbone, George?" Charlie Dalton asked.

"Oh, one of these days when there's a long spell that I don't have anything else to do."

Reynolds' sally brought general laughter and hooting. Nearly all the men knew Reynolds; he usually had more irons in the fire than a branding crew. But years later, on July 17, 1882, he did have the arrowhead removed. Three surgeons— Drs. Lewis and Griffith of Kansas City and Dr. Powell of New York City—performed the operation in a Kansas City hospital.

Now Reynolds shouted across the room to Charlie Dalton, "Charlie, why don't you tell us how your pa hid that $15,000 on that last trip he made to Kansas?"

It took some persuasion to get the story out, but it came. Charlie's father, M. L. Dalton, had moved to Texas from Tennessee after marrying a girl from Kentucky. He and his wife had started their ranch in Palo Pinto County with seventy cattle purchased with gold given Mrs. Dalton by her father. The herd increased rapidly, but later it was often raided by Indians. In 1866, M. L. Dalton trailed eight hundred cattle to New Mexico and came home with $16,000. The next year he drove one thousand to the same place and this time received $22,000. In 1868, he changed direction and trailed five hundred head to Kansas and sold them for $6,000.

Dalton was paid in gold for his cattle. Since there were no banks or other safe places of deposit in his part of the country, he buried the money on his ranch.

He made his second trip to Kansas in 1869 and sold six hundred good steers for $15,000.

"It wasn't $15,000 Pa started home with," Charlie told the men around the Richards House stove. "It was $11,500. Pa had bought two new wagons, provisions for the ranch, and two new trunks, which, knowing Ma's and the girls' dreams of finery, he had filled with new clothes for them."

Only a few miles from home, Dalton and two of his men, James Redfield and Jim McCaster, were killed and scalped. The Indians took the teams, wagons and supplies.

"The Indians made off with everything," Charlie related. "But they threw away one of the trunk trays beside the trail. It didn't have anything in it but an old shoe. We looked in the shoe, and there was the money. Pa had taken it in green-backs that time."

It was right after Dalton's death that Mrs. Dalton sold the rest of her cattle to Jim Loving.

This well-known fact led to talk of Loving and his ups and downs in the cow business. When his father was killed on the Pecos in 1867, Jim had to take over. The father and his partner, Charles Goodnight, had a good many cattle in Texas, and to settle the partnership, Jim had to drive them to Colorado to sell—over one of the most dangerous of Western trails.

After making preparation for the drive, Jim Loving rode back to Weatherford to say good-by to his wife and children, for he had little idea that he would see them again. While he was on this mission home, Indians raided his trail outfit and stole nearly all the horses.

After going to the expense and trouble of getting more horses, Loving started for Colorado on June 20, 1868. L. E. and Milton Ikard, Mode and John Kutch, Fayette Wilson and John H. Caruthers had small bunches in the herd, which with

the Loving and Goodnight cows numbered twenty-three
hundred. These six men planned to ride through as hands
and sell their cattle in Colorado.

A herd owned and driven by Simpson Crawford, W. R.
and J. C. Curtis and Charles E. Rivers followed the Loving
and Goodnight outfit. In the Indian Territory, John H.
Caruthers cut out from the Loving and Goodnight herd and

returned home. Charley Rivers from the other herd decided to do the same thing. Then in western Kansas, Crawford and the Ikard boys sold their cattle to Loving. The two herds, now consolidated, numbered nearly four thousand head. After this business deal, Crawford, the Ikard brothers and Henry Kutch, who had become ill, returned to Texas. The drive west on the old Santa Fe road continued under the management and control of Jim Loving.

— HDBugbee —

Out on an open plain near a great bend of the Arkansas River, Loving warned his men to be on the lookout, for they were in the land where the Comanches and Kiowas spent the summer season. The warning had hardly been passed down the long line from one cowboy to another when about a mile ahead Loving saw a band of some fifteen hundred mounted Indians stretched across the trail and formed, to all appearances, in line of battle.

Quickly the men in the outfit gathered around Loving to ask what they could do. The cattle ambled unconcernedly on toward the warriors. Loving told the cowboys to fall back to the wagons that carried provisions. There were about twenty men, all well armed.

At the wagons each man got all the cartridges he could manage.

"We'll wait to see what the Indians do now," Loving said. "If we try to run, they'll kill us sure. Our horses are tired and theirs are fresh, and anyway there's no place to run. We'll put up a bold front. If we have to fight, sell out as dearly as possible."

The cattle slowed to a stop. Three of the Indians rode out from the main army to the cowboys and asked for their chief. Jim Loving was pointed out, and he went over to them. One of the Indians was a Comanche chief named Black Beaver; another was a Mexican half-breed. In the cowboy outfit was a man named Calhoun who could speak the Mexican language. Those two acted as interpreters. The Indians wanted to know if the herd and men were from Texas, for, the half-breed said, the Comanches were on the warpath with *Tehanas* (Texans).

Calhoun talked fast. The men, he said, were from western Kansas and had been down in the Cherokee Nation and had bought the cattle there. The cattle were for the government under contract, he told them.

Black Beaver gave instructions that the cattle could go on; they would not be bothered.

The Mexican later told Calhoun that Indians, out killing buffalo, had seen the dust from the herd a long distance away and had thought them to be an army of Osages. The Comanches were on the warpath with that tribe and the fifteen hundred Indians the cowboys saw had come out to do battle with the Osages and prevent them from getting to where their squaws and papooses were encamped a few miles up the Arkansas River.

No Texas cowboy bones of that outfit bleached on the prairie. The drive continued and on September 14, 1868, reached the Loving and Goodnight ranch on the Apishapaw in Colorado.

Someone reminisced about a man who was killed and scalped by a Comanche and yet had been buried with his scalp on after all. Out on a remote ranch the victim had been chopping wood when a lone warrior slithered up and shot an arrow into his heart. Then he took the man's scalp and hurried away. The man's partner found the bloody body and tracked the Indian brave all night. He returned the middle of the next afternoon with his friend's scalp plus the scalp of the Comanche for good measure. As he drove into the ranch yard, the murdered cowman's funeral was just ending. The partner carefully patted the top of his friend's head back in place.

"It was the principle of the thing," George Reynolds explained. "The way I heard it, that fellow was bald-headed."

Despite the scars of an era that was blessedly gone, perhaps the most peculiarly marked cowman in the circle of gentlemen characterized by their past, present or potential eminence was an Irishman named J. C. Lynch on whose ranch depredations of the new era started.

He could tell with colorful embellishments the story that pretty definitely established the fact that cattle rustling as a lock-stock-and-barrel business had started on the Lynch Ranch on Hubbard Creek in Shackelford County.

Lynch had made his way to the cattle frontier by the most circuitous of routes. An adventurer at heart, the jolly Lynch had come to Hubbard Creek from his native Ireland via the gold rush in California. In his seven years of gold hunting he kept hearing that Texas was a lively place, and he decided it was the place for him. He headed eastward. In Mesilla County, Arizona, he met Dr. Peter Gonzolus and his family—moving westward to California. The instant Lynch set eyes on pretty Frances Gonzolus he fell head over heels in love with her and he married her there in Arizona a few days later. He thereby changed the course of his life and the direction of travel of Frances' family; her parents turned around and journeyed to Texas with the newlyweds, stopping in Fort Griffin. Lynch and Frances found a place they liked out on Hubbard Creek and there they set up housekeeping in a dugout. Lynch prospered as a cowman, with a wide grassy range, good cattle and a fine two-story white house for Frances Gonzolus Lynch.

How this Irishman happened to be the first victim of serious cattle rustling is the story of the early developments of the beef business and of the Southwest and, to some extent, the Middle West. The men in the hotel lobby were involved in a major way in that story.

Soon after the Texas Revolution, which ended in victory for the Texans at the Battle of San Jacinto in 1836, men like George Webb Slaughter, the father of C. C. Slaughter, began dealing in cattle. These were wild, tough beasts which had descended from early imports from Spain. George Slaughter, a native of Tennessee, had moved to Texas before the Texas Revolution and was Gen. Sam Houston's right-hand man in that struggle. Slaughter was the last man to deliver a message to the Alamo. He was the first man to marry under the laws of the Texas Republic, and his son, C. C., was the first child born of a Texas Republic marriage.

In the days of the Texas Republic and of early statehood, which came in 1845, the cattle business flourished, but mainly as an industry of hoofs, horns, hides and tallow. Richard King, a sea captain who had migrated from New York State, bought his vast King Ranch and imported stock cattle from Mexico in 1853. In order to market his herds he had to put in a rendering plant on his ranch.

By this time, George Slaughter, displaying that characteristic that has been evident in all generations of cowmen, felt the urge for room, and he moved to the Indian-ravaged frontier. He was a Baptist preacher and a practical doctor of medicine. In Slaughter Valley among the shapely hills of Palo Pinto County, Slaughter preached the gospel, married young lovers, delivered their babies, doctored the sick, buried the dead, fought the Indians, raised cattle and reared a family of eleven children.

Even before the Civil War, some Texans were trailing cattle to Missouri, Kansas and Illinois in search of markets. During that war the cattle went largely unattended on the unfenced grasslands. Arriving home after Appomattox, still Rebels, but penniless Rebels, the Texans found it hard to get back in harness and make a living. But the Spanish cattle had increased while the battles raged to the southeast, and they now crowded the range. If there were only a market for these critters! That was the universal thought in Texas. So the Waggoners, Slaughters, Burnetts, Lovings, along with their neighbors and their contemporaries of the range across Texas, hit the trails—California, the Gulf States, Missouri, Illinois, Kansas, Wyoming. Of all these places, Kansas proved to be the most convenient and profitable market, and by 1867 the trails to Kansas were established.

It was then that Joseph B. McCoy, a promotion-minded livestock shipper of Illinois, had a brilliant dream that appealed to Texans. Observing the herds on the Texas trails, McCoy decided there ought to be a central market in Kansas, on a railroad running to the heavily populated areas of the North and East. So McCoy established Abilene, on the Kansas Pacific Railroad. He put up stock pens and loading facilities and built a hotel for the trail men. He invited Texans to market in Abilene, and this arrangement suited them.

The first Texas cattle shipped out of Abilene, the first really wild and woolly cowtown, were trailed there by C. C. Slaughter.

Abilene boomed as the star of the trail until 1871, during which summer nearly half a million Texas longhorns bawled and milled on the Kansas prairie, and there were no buyers; there was simply no demand for cattle at any price. In order to save their herds and try to get something out of them, many of the Texans drove westward and northward into lands they didn't know. In this way, Texas cattle were driven into nearly all the Western states—New Mexico, Wyoming, Montana, the Dakotas—and were the first beef cattle to replace buffaloes on many a wide sweep of range. The debacle of 1871 killed Abilene as a cattle market.

But the die-hard Texans kept driving to Kansas, and Dodge City, on to the west of Abilene, began taking shape as a thriving trail town. Then the ranchers were jolted again—this time almost fatally—in 1873 when panic, which started in the financial centers of the East, spread across the country.

That fall and winter, tens of thousands of Texas cattle died on the snow-swept Kansas prairies.

By this time the cowmen realized that their enterprise seemed destined to be a boom and bust business, but they didn't let that throw them; they stuck to it.

And sticking straight in the saddle were the Lynches on Hubbard Creek telling each other, "B'gorra, it will be *bueno* next year."

Not far away the big guns of the hunters boomed on the buffalo plains in perhaps the greatest wholesale slaughter of wild animals known to the world. This bloody harvest of the shaggy beasts attracted hundreds of men—shooters, skinners, freighters, and a good many of them were riffraff from all over the country.

Fort Griffin flourished mightily as the buffalo capital. Hunting expeditions organized and supplied there; then vast loads of buffalo skins were hauled into Griffin for relay to eastern points. In a single year, more than a million buffalo hides were hauled over the trail from Griffin to Dodge City in enormous freight wagons, each pulled by ten yokes of straining oxen.

Griffin grew into a little hub of an almost endless universe, with trails spoking out in every direction—east to Graham, northwest to Fort Sill, southwest to Fort Concho (near San Angelo, Texas), and the main trail north and west to Dodge City. This route was almost as famous as the Old Chisholm itself.

So Griffin became the den of itinerant, well-armed rogues.

When the buffalo herds were all slain and their bones lay bleaching under the scorching sun, these men were out of work, and cowboy wages of two tens and a five every month plus keep didn't appeal to them. So it was that the buffalo men —mainly the skinners—joined by a few renegade army deserters, ganged up one dark night in Griffin, rode out to the

Lynch Ranch and drove off a herd of cattle. And that was the start of rustling as an industrial art, which spread like wildfire all over those rangelands and broke, or badly bent, men like Jim Loving.

Always there had been a dribble of cattle stealing in the past. Besides the raiding Indians and men long on rope but short on integrity, border bandits had made life miserable on ranches, such as that of Captain King, along the Rio Grande. Men who lost cattle and horses to the Indians or had them stolen and driven across into Mexico could apply for reparations from the federal government. But those who lost to the new brand of rustlers had no one to whom they could appeal; theirs were definite losses.

There had grown up in the Southwest the accepted practice of mavericking—getting loops on unbranded animals past the weaning age. But this had been gentlemanly theft. In the days before the 1870's, horse stealing was the unforgivable sin, and it was an honor to be in a mob that proudly strung up a hoss thief. At the same time, the mavericker and even the man who drove off a few of a distant neighbor's cows could still serve as deacon or play dominoes with the high sheriff. Some ranchers were "cow poor" and actually were obliged by the men who reduced herds by a few stolen head. Cattle stealing had barely been recognized by the lawmakers; on the law books it was a misdemeanor only, and the thief who was caught could pay a small fine and go his way without deep disgrace.

But the buffalo men and their wholesale ways changed all this. Cattle losses ran high, and cowmen hurried to their legislators. However, it was not until 1873 that cattle stealing was made a felony—only four years before the meeting at Graham.

After the successful start of rustling on Hubbard Creek,

the thieves continually grew bolder. They were credited with running out of the country a cavalier of the range, the most dashing of cowmen—John Chisum. After battling the cutthroat rustlers in Texas, Chisum decided to head his herds westward, driving into the untrammeled lands along the Pecos in the Territory of New Mexico. He was one of the first major cattlemen to try that region.

Chisum, tall, dark and handsome, with a waxed mustache curled neatly at the ends, liked the spectacular and the surprising. His brand—the Fence Rail—was a long, narrow burn from neck to flank, but it was not marked for fame. However, the Chisum earmark was the most widely known in the West. Chisum cut the ears of his cattle so that the middle section hung down and the rest of the ear stood up. This hanging flap bobbed around like the clapper of a bell, and so it was that Chisum's cattle were called the Jinglebobs.

Stealing on an ambitious commercial scale could be accomplished successfully because of the wide, unpeopled expanse of the cattlelands and also because long, strung-out herds of cattle were moved over winding trails to market. The region which concerned the men at Graham, known generally as northwest Texas, was invitingly situated for the propagation of range dishonesty. It covered almost one-third of the big state. To the north, across Red River, lay the Indian Territory, now Oklahoma; to the west and north rose the stark buffalo plains, and still farther west was the untamed Territory of New Mexico. In the vastness of northwest Texas there was only one telegraph line, and to the frontier families the long, slender landmark was referred to as "the telegraph." Out on the treeless plains, now known as the Panhandle, only one county had been organized and had a sheriff; it was Wheeler County, the site of the only military outpost for many long miles—Fort Elliott. On its long north and west lines, Texas joined no state, but Indian- and outlaw-infested territories, generally unorganized and many years from statehood.

By its annexation treaty with the United States, Texas, the only state that was ever an independent republic, kept and controlled its vast public domain, which was wide open; all who desired to do so used the land, the grass and the waterholes. In all of the other western states, the federal government owned and managed the public domain and, therefore, the range was under the surveillance of Washington agencies and was never wholly free as was the land in Texas, where cowmen drove their herds wherever they pleased. There was no red tape involving use of the Texas grassland—just gentlemanly understanding between herdsmen, who respected each other's established range.

In the late spring, the trail herds that originated in the older ranchlands of Texas—down in the southern part of the state—crossed this wide, undulating country of northwest Texas, forded Red River with its floods and treacherous quicksands and then grazed across the Indian country to northern markets.

It was easy for rustlers to ride in and drive off whole herds; it was likewise easy for the thieves to sneak their stolen stock to market or to distant ranges in New Mexico; or they could sell, with one hundred per cent profit and a minimum risk of detection, to the big outfits from far away as they trailed, one after the other, across this part of the country.

In 1873, William Hittson, a Texas cowman who was known as "Colonel John," was commissioned by northwest Texas stock growers to raid the Territory of New Mexico in search of stolen cattle. Armed with powers of attorney given him by cowmen to take charge of any stock bearing their brands and also otherwise armed, Hittson rode into New Mexico, taking along three picked men. This cow frontier patrol worked silently, riding the range and spotting cattle. Within a year, Hittson and his men recovered ten thousand cattle that had been stolen in Texas and herded across the plains.

But such an operation was only a drop in the bucket; it didn't even discourage the thieves. Neither could the spasmodic hanging of rustlers break up such a lucrative enterprise.

The cattlemen in session in Graham were accordingly in a lather. Also it might have been that they had a portent of impending events. There were many straws in the west wind that were blowing toward change—big and little.

Several of the cowmen had heard a fantastic tale about a fellow named H. B. Sanborn of Illinois coming to Texas to introduce a new thing called barbed wire.

Burk Burnett wore a big white hat that was the envy of all. John B. Stetson's headgear, which he had designed in Philadelphia and named the Boss of the Plains, was just making its bow as the crowning glory of western stockmen.

Texas cowmen were acquiring more of their own deeded land—buying their grass instead of depending wholly on the open range. Earlier only men like Captain King had bothered to buy their elbow room. Nearly all the ranchers in Richards House owned land. Some of the men had heard that Bill Day of Austin, long a free-grass rancher and a trail driver of note, had bought twenty thousand acres out in Coleman County in western Texas.

The discussion of land brought out reports that capitalists in the British Isles had been sending representatives to the American West to check on fabulous stories of rich promise in land and cattle empires.

Only two years before, Texans had voted into their constitution a provision to swap three million acres in one tract for the building of a fine state capitol.

W. S. Ikard told of a big event he had attended in Philadelphia the year before. It was the Centennial Exposition there, and stockmen had seen something new and promising— white-faced cattle called Herefords. Ikard had struck up with a southern Texas trail driver, Ike Pryor, and together they had taken a gander at the Herefords. The new cattle looked good to Ikard, and on his way home he had stopped in Illinois and bought ten young Hereford bulls for spring delivery. They would reach him by rail, over the new line of the Missouri, Kansas and Texas (Katy) Railroad, which had reached Texas in 1872. His bulls, Ikard said, would be unloaded at Denison (now celebrated as the birthplace of President Eisenhower), and he would drive them to his ranch just northwest of Graham. Ikard was the first to ship Herefords into Texas.

What was to become of Texas cattle, the leathery, durable longhorns that had already lost caste outside the confines of big Texas? C. C. Slaughter vowed that there would be a more profitable breed or type. He told of his experience with Shorthorns. A couple of years before, he had bought about four thousand carefully selected heifers; then he had gone to Kentucky and bought Shorthorn bulls. Therefore, he was the first cowman in Texas to try something besides the old, reliable longhorn.

One of the men in the circle popped up and said he didn't know about the new-fangled stuff, arguing that the Spanish cattle had been in Texas since the Year One and had done all right. He told of Col. Tom Shannon, who back in 1848 had brought in two Durham cows and a bull fresh from Queen Victoria's own herd. Colonel Tom had thought so much of these royal bovines that when they were unloaded off the boat at New Orleans, he hauled them up to north Texas in wagons. "The way I look at it," the cowman decided, "a man has no business with cows that can't light out and walk from New Orleans."

George Reynolds rose to defend the Durham, or Shorthorn, maintaining that the breed was the coming one for Texas. Two years before, Reynolds had brought in Durham cows and bulls from Colorado. He told the group that the Katy Railroad had already hauled something over two hundred carloads of breeding cattle into Texas.

Those Texans who now talked of importing better breeds of cattle had, with their enterprise with longhorns, almost wiped out beef production in the original cow country of this nation—New England and the area around New York and Philadelphia. In these Northern and Eastern provinces cattle had to be fed and sheltered in the winter. Moreover, land prices were too high for great herds to be grazed profitably. But Texas had its boundless grasslands where cattle could graze the year around and live and fatten without feed or expensive barns. Therefore, the East could not compete in beef raising with this new territory where land was free or dirt cheap, although the East had had the fine breeds of beef cattle all along.

Actually, beef cattle—breeds far superior to the bawling Spanish longhorn—had come to America with the early colonists, and the first great cow country in the nation was the Connecticut Valley.

As early as 1624, small herds were imported into New England from Devonshire in old England by Governor Winslow. Capt. John Mason (a forebear of C. C. Slaughter's mother) bought cattle in Denmark and shipped them to New Hampshire. These were large yellow bovines. One day in 1638 about one hundred oxen of this breed were trailed into Boston, where they sold at twenty-five pounds sterling each.

Some forgotten "firsts" in the beef business occurred in the Connecticut Valley near Springfield, Massachusetts. There William Pynchon became a big-scale trail driver. He was the first beef-cattle feeder, and he trailed his fat steers into Boston, where the marketplace in 1655 was on the site where the state house now stands. Moreover, Pynchon was America's first packer, his plant having been located near Springfield.

Cattle from Holland were imported by the Dutch to the vicinity of New York City. They fattened on the grass thereabouts and were slaughtered at a place just below Wall Street. By 1695, about four thousand cattle were being slaughtered there, and on the Brooklyn shore, each year.

In Pennsylvania, the Quakers and Germans were among the first feeders of beef cattle, and Philadelphia was the main seaboard market and shipping point—before the American Revolution.

Shorthorns were introduced in Virginia as early as 1783 by Goff and Miller, who grazed their cattle on blue grass and fed them on Indian corn. The progeny of these cattle went with settlers into Ohio and Kentucky, and herds of big steers were trailed across the mountains to the markets of Philadelphia and Baltimore.

Col. Lewis Sanders made a historic importation of Shorthorns into Kentucky in 1817. He had read of a great English bull named Comet that had sold at auction for a thousand guineas. And he imported a herd of that bloodline from the Teeswater Valley.

These cattle moved westward with the pioneers—to Indiana, Illinois, Missouri, the edge of Kansas. And the raising of beef was one of the first enterprises of the early settlers of the Midwestern Corn Belt. In that region—especially in Illinois and Missouri—there were great cattle barons long before Texas cowboys ever started chasing longhorns.

But now the land of the longhorn had won its spurs as the natural cow country, in which the industry had developed from almost nothing within fewer than twenty years. At last, the long-avoided, high and dry buffalo plains had cattle. C. C. Slaughter related news of this, saying that Charlie Goodnight was testing the Panhandle. Except for T. S. Bugbee, who had followed him by a few months, Goodnight had the whole vast windy world up there to himself. He had ranched first around Palo Pinto County, blazed trails across Texas, New Mexico and Colorado, and finally established a ranch in Colorado. Now he had returned to Texas, driving his herd from Colorado and settling in the Palo Duro Canyon, a chasm in the face of the level plains, the start of Red River. With Jim Loving's father, Goodnight had blazed the first cattle trails across western Texas and New Mexico. The men that night at Graham didn't know that in the future big-scale range wars, this powerful man on the buffalo plains would stand, well-Winchestered, against them.

Talk of Goodnight and the cattle trails brought up the subject of the baffling mystery of Texas cattle. For years, all the way back to the first drives, Texas cattle had been thought to possess devils which crawled out in other states and killed local cattle. In Kansas, Missouri, Illinois and other states, when native cattle grazed behind herds from Texas, the native cattle died in vast numbers. As a consequence, nearly every other state, even faraway New York, had at one time or another slammed a ban on Texas longhorns. And no one knew why other cattle died when they grazed behind Texas herds.

Some superstitious ones argued that an ancient Spanish curse hexed the longhorns. Others were sure that a mystery shrub in Texas wounded the feet of cattle, making sores that leaked poison on the grass. Another colorful diagnosis was that Texas cattle, with their distended nostrils, were infected with a poisonous halitosis.

The cattlemen were in Graham to make campaign plans

for war on the rustler, but these other things also concerned them.

Between the time of the strife among the cow waddies of Abraham and Lot, as recorded in the Bible, and the meeting under the oak at Graham, as recorded in the scrawling handwriting of Jim Loving, there had been little of record to show any tendency toward organization among stockmen. But this meeting in Graham brought home the fact that on the frontier of America the age of the lone wolf was passing.

· 3 ·

A Sort of Acorn

With admirable terseness and a dynamic spirit, the committee reported on its proposals next morning when again the forty men met under the oak. Chairman Carter asked Loving to read the proposals.

The suggested name of the new organization was the Stock Raisers Association of Northwestern Texas, Loving reported. Then he read from the proposed resolutions:

First. That the members of this association shall work together for the good and common interest of the stock raisers of northwestern Texas and do all in their power for the promotion of the stock interest.

Second. That the territory represented at this convention be divided into districts and that men be allotted to each district whose duty it shall be to gather all cattle in their district and to notify the owners of the same and hold them until owners call for them.

Another chore of the committee had been that of laying off the territory into the half-a-dozen districts and assigning members to oversee each one. It is doubtful whether there is an old cowman left alive—or even whether there is a surveyor —who could figure out the metes and bounds of those first districts, for at that time men went by landmarks and they were all familiar with the lines given. The boundaries of No. 1 District were designated this way:

51

Commencing at the mouth of Keechie Creek, at its junction with the Brazos River, and running on a line to Cement Mountain; thence south to the Brazos River near the old agency, and down the Brazos to the point of commencement.

The second was as picturesquely designated:

Commencing at the north corner of No. 1 and running to the mouth of Lodge Creek in West Fork to its head; thence south to where the telegraph crosses Dry Creek . . .

With their boundaries described on the basis of meandering streams, waterholes and ranch headquarters, the six districts sprawled across northern Texas from almost the northeast corner where the state joins Arkansas far westward past the Double Mountain country nearly to El Paso. The northern line was along Red River. The territory of the new association's self-assumed authority didn't extend to the Panhandle since only Goodnight and a few new neighbors were operating in that part of the world.

The district system was a good working idea since it set up a line of detection and protection across the territory. One of its greatest advantages would be during the all-important roundup—the work in spring and fall when the herds mingling on the open, unfenced range were gathered so that each owner could claim his stock as identified by his brand. The members in each district were charged with the job of picking the man to direct this roundup work. On the roundup, if there was doubt as to ownership of one cow or a herd or a question on whether brands had been changed, the decision was up to the roundup boss; this was a universal law of the range. Although only an hour old, the Association had sufficient membership in each district to boss the roundup.

Grazing cows would pay no attention to imaginary district

lines; they would cross Keechie Creek if green grass led in that direction, browse along the flinty foot of Cement Mountain and never pause for the shadow of the telegraph line where it crossed Dry Creek, but in whatever district the cattle might roam, there would be Association members to see about them for their fellow members. In order to do this, the members had to know each other's brand and marks, and, therefore, Secretary Loving was handed his first big chore—getting up a brand book.

This new system was due for a test fairly soon. In late spring, the trail herds from southern and central Texas would be passing that way. There would be Association members to look over these herds and make sure that stock belonging to other members hadn't become—accidentally or on purpose —mixed in with the traveling beeves. Formerly, if a rustler rounded up a bunch of steers—say, from J. C. Lynch—and tried to sell them to a trail outfit at a price below market, the trail boss, recognizing a bargain, had no way of knowing the cattle were stolen, and to Kansas and market they plodded. Under the new system, members in each district would watch trail herds for evidence of such deals, and they could take over the "hot" stock. Though the organization was intended to combat outright professional thieves, the cowmen, now that they were organized, could keep a weather eye on local brethren as well. Dwelling reputably in the midst of the stockmen were gentlemen whose conscience had the elasticity of a golden girl's garter. From all outward appearance, they were upright and law-abiding men; they mouthed loudly their inherent abhorrence of rustlers, cutthroats and scoundrels of all schools. Such an operator could round up his own stock and maybe not notice that a fair-sized bunch belonging to someone else had been included. When such a "mistake" was called to his attention, he was always the soul of innocence. "I'm sorry as hell," he would apologize. "Cut them strays, boys. Sure glad you noticed it. Sure am."

The cowmen wanted to make life miserable for such neighbors.

A policy of honest dealing was the acorn planted there under the old Graham oak.

". . . and do all in their power for the promotion of the stock interest"—that was the heart of the thing. Cowmen believed that the welfare of the world was in good shape only when the stock interest had been properly protected.

The new association elected Kit Carter its first president, and Jim Loving was picked for the only pay job—that of secretary—at fifty dollars a year. The vice-president was J. D. Smith, and S. J. Conner was made assistant secretary.

Carter was re-elected year after year and, with the exception of one year when he was ill and C. C. Slaughter filled his boots, served the Association as top man for eleven years. Loving's ability as an executive and his know-how in the cattle business kept him in office until after the turn of the century.

The men who headed their districts were: C. L. Carter, the Slaughter brothers, Thomas Scarborough, T. J. Atkinson, Charles Dalton and D. C. Kyle for district one; G. G. Milliken, the Wilson brothers, B. R. Willett, J. C. Loving, H. G. Bedford and W. C. Hunt for district two; J. H. Graham, J. T. Farrar, J. W. Medlan, J. S. and D. W. Godwin, J. D. Smith, E. C. Davis, George Terrell, A. B. Medlan, N. H. Graham, McCommis and Hunt, C. C. Mills, W. B. Mills, John Stevens, T. H. Brummett, R. E. Mabry, Hardesty, Boar and Company, L. L. Clark, Carpenter and Eaton, John W. Proffitt, R. J. Johnson and Wright and Brothers for district three;

Waggoner and Son, Harrold Brothers, Ikard Brothers, Halsell
Brothers, Curtis Brothers, Millett Brothers, Stephen and
Worsham, Reed and Day, Flippins and Merchant, S. B. Bur-
nett, J. J. Lang, Lute Renshaw, John Dawson, Strong, W. S.
Brown, F. M. Goodwin, S. A. Belcher, A. W. Crawford,
B. B. Scarborough and Joe Bryant for district four; W. E.
Stewart, Roberts Brothers, A. J. and F. M. Long, J. W. Frury,
Clayton and Cowen, E. Martin, John Hullum, Carter and
Grounds and Couts and Simpson for district five; and J. F.
Webb, John Hittson, John Millsap, George Gambell, W. S.
Dyer, C. L. Wasson, Willis Benson and William Hullum for
district six.

The cowmen, the resolutions of their first convention
adopted, adjourned after agreeing to meet again in April in
Graham to complete rules for the spring roundup and to pro-
ceed with other active business.

Virginia-born Kit Carter with his fortitude and daring
courage was a fine choice for president, since he was a man
the others respected and one who had shoulders wide enough
and a whitening head wise enough to bear the responsibilities
of leading an organization whose members were unused to
working in harness.

In 1855, Carter and his wife had left the peaceful and
civilized village of Waco on the lower Brazos and headed up
the river. They had ridden on the springy seat of a covered
wagon that held their household possessions and the first of
their children, who one day would number eleven. They had
followed the winding river with its precious supply of water
until in a faraway virgin valley at the most treacherous bend
in the river's course they had found the spot Carter once had
seen on a horseback trip. Few white men had ever ventured
there since its shaded canyons, tall spotted oaks and thick

underbrush afforded perfect stomping grounds for the Indians, who preferred to pitch their tepees close to flowing water also. Carter was a highly skilled rifleman and he had trusted in his ability to look after his family. He had many opportunities to use his rifle, for Indians constantly raided his herds and many times threatened harm to his wife and children.

The Carters named their home "Carter's Bend." Their nearest neighbor, when they moved there, was thirty miles away, not counting the unneighborly red men, and their mail still came to Waco. At first the house was a long, low log cabin with a veranda all the way across the front. Later an adjoining two-story frame addition was built and two tall chimneys extended up as high as the surrounding trees.

Mrs. Carter had trusted in her ability to make a home in this beautiful but dangerous wilderness. Before she married Kit Carter in 1843, she had been Ann Ross, sister of Sul Ross, the most famous of Texas Indian scouts. This brother was elected Governor of Texas in 1886.

Indians and rustlers, and even tragedy that saddened them the rest of their lives, couldn't drive the Carters from their ranch in the bend of the Brazos. They were stayers.

On a March morning in 1869, the Carters' son, Shapley, and eleven other cowboys were working six miles from Graham. A band of fifty roving Indians surrounded them, and the boys opened up with their pistols. The Indians charged with long-range rifles and flying arrows. In the fight that lasted all day, one cowboy was killed and six others were wounded—two of them fatally. Shapley Carter was hit in the side with a poisoned arrow, and he died that night. He was buried on a hill above his home and the granite stone at his head was chiseled to read:

S. P. Carter
Born
Aug. 2, 1847
Died
March 18, 1869
Killed by Indians

The grass had greened on the range where Shapley Carter and the cowboys had fought eight springs before when Kit Carter rode over it on his way back to Graham for the April meeting of the new cattle association.

Again the lobby of the Richards House swarmed with men. Members of the Association learned that the rest of the state's stockmen hadn't left the business of trying to prevent cattle theft entirely up to them.

In March, three men had stolen a bunch of steers in Grayson County, to the east of Graham, and had driven them to a point near the Arkansas line and sold them at one hundred per cent profit. Since this venture clicked so well, the men had helped themselves to more steers there and returned with them to Grayson County. Again they had made a profitable sale, and, feeling businesslike, they offered a bill of sale. While this document was being drawn, the rightful owners of the cattle showed up. With no whereases or wherefores, they marched the three thieves out to a tree near Goose Pond and strung them up in a neat row.

To each dead rustler's shirt was fastened a tall-lettered placard reading:

Cattle Thieves' Doom

Members from around Hubbard Creek and Fort Griffin reported that citizens of Fort Griffin had formed a vigilance committee which had put itself under sworn oath to take im-

— HDBugbee —

mediate care of horse and cow thieves, and also to look after the community's morals in general.

The northwest Texas cowmen had some dirty linen of their own to wash at this second session. One of the charter members was accused of violating rules against driving, molesting and disturbing cattle not in his own district. At the request of a committee elected to look into the charge, President Carter administered a public reprimand to the member, in which he emphasized that no man would ever be permitted to use his membership as a shield to hide wrongdoing.

Then, in frank words, the Association announced its intention of controlling all movements of livestock within the bounds of its vast territory. This resolution, offered by Capt. E. B. Millett, was loudly approved:

> That on all routes where cattle are being driven out of the country [meaning out of the state to market], *strict watch* should be kept in the interest of all by those nearest to said trails, and should assistance be needed in stopping any herd or in arresting any parties who are driving cattle from their accustomed range, it will be so given by one or all of us if necessary.

Thus sworn to fight as individuals or as a group any trail outfit that picked up strays or bought from thieves and mingled the stolen cows into a moving herd, the cowmen rode away from the oak and Graham to their spring roundups.

In each of the six districts the wagons, the men, the horses gathered at the designated central place. The chuck wagons groaned with loads of supplies—food, bedding, branding irons, water kegs. Every rancher in the district sent an outfit, and within a couple of days, the sprawling camp was alive with men, who loafed and talked while waiting for more distant outfits to roll in.

The roundup boss was selected—of course, a member of the Association—and the work started. The men rode in wide circles, gradually closing in and bringing the cattle in the surrounded area together. Then came the cutting, the calf branding, the steering of bull calves. As always, the identity of the calf that pranced at the side or nuzzled the flank of a cow was established by the brand on the cow. As the stock were worked, the cattle were bunched; the steers and the cull cows that were going to market—up the Chisholm—were put in one herd; the mother cows and the calves were turned loose to go back to grazing on the area that had been worked.

Day after day the men rode, circling, gathering, cutting. The cumbersome chuck wagons kept pace with the riders, the cooks selecting camping places where there were wood and water. Campfires, tall tales, night guard, rainstorms with vivid lightning, swollen creeks, old Red River on a toot—these were the hallmarks of the roundup.

The work, routine for cow outfits, was easy until the visitors began arriving. On any night from late spring until early summer, campfires glowed, one within sight of the next, across Texas from Red River to San Antonio and the Rio.

Captain King's longhorns, strung out for miles in several herds, came grazing through, with Anglo-Saxon bosses and sombreroed *vaqueros*. The outfits had provisioned in Fort Worth and pulled into the vicinity of Red River Station in the present Montague County—a few degrees west of north of Fort Worth.

The Red, fed by the freshets of Texas and the Indian country, was rolling swiftly three hundred yards wide, deep and dirty-looking in the middle. The drovers would wait for the river to run down a bit.

A trail outfit of Lytle and McDaniel camped nearby.

Ike Pryor was on the trail—the first time as an owner. He had two hundred and fifty cattle in a herd belonging to John W. Gamel. This outfit took a look at the Red and decided to wait a few days. Before long, a wide territory up and down the river was covered with cattle, horses, wagons.

At night the cowboys gathered around the campfires except for the ones left on watch, whose duty it was to ride around and around the cattle bunched and bedded down and to look for strays that might decide to get hay or a drink of water while the moon was shining. These nomads were quickly caught by the boys and pushed back into the herd. Slowly the cowboy walked his horse, for the cool night air was refreshing after the heat of the day. With a big puff, as if all the air had suddenly escaped from a balloon, a large steer settled down on his side. After a while all the animals had quieted down into gently breathing dark shadows. Overhead the stars were bright and occasionally a muted laugh was carried on the breeze from the group around the dying campfire.

One outfit had hired a cook in Fort Worth. He was a young man who had done little cooking but was willing to try any sort of work in order to get a trail trip. One evening the boss told him to stew dried apples. He heaped his stewer, poured it rim-full of water and put it on the fire. Taking on the moisture and heat, the apples swelled, rose high above the edge of the pot and began to roll off into the fire. Some of the hands—they reported around a chuck wagon that night— watched the new cook. Quickly he dug a hole behind a small clump of brush and buried the spilled-over apples there, working fast in an effort to keep anyone from noticing his inexperience. Next morning the boys nicknamed him Apple Jack.

Another cook in one of the outfits had a bantam rooster along, a bright, perky little fellow with long, curving feathers in its tail and a blood-red comb. Someone had given the chicken to the trail boss, and the cook kept it in a net-wire cage at the wagon. The little rooster feasted on scraps. Like the men, the chicken adapted himself to the life of the trail and the cow camp, and, rooster-like, he kept a certain schedule. With the first light of the approaching dawn the rooster announced the coming of another day. He crowed with all his might, challengingly. But there were no answers; this rooster was too far from any farms to be heard. But he did set off other sounds—the neighing of horses; the belching and swallowing of cows waking up, bovine bones and joints popping as the herds stirred; cows bawling; chain harness swinging in the breeze against wagon wheels; the rattle of pots and pans; the crackle of wood fires and the sizzling of bacon.

The cockiness of the little rooster inspired a good deal of cow-camp comment. Not only did he shrilly greet the dawn; he let loose at midnight. Some of the greenhorn punchers on their first trail trip complained of work on third guard at night, saying that the nightmarish crowing of the rooster made the cattle nervous and hard to hold.

But bowlegged old-timers set the youngsters straight. Cows, they explained, were always restless at midnight. The veteran punchers called it the witching hour—when the cattle stirred and half-awakened as if they had a special sense that called them to be up and about when in the middle of the night one day blended into another.

Late one afternoon an outfit with a herd of "buggered" steers showed up and made camp several hundred yards away from any other wagon. But the cowboys wandered from campfire to campfire and talked. The steers of this new outfit were nervous from trouble the previous night. Lightning from a quick spring thunderstorm had stampeded them, but the men had managed to mill and hold them. Darkness had settled down by the time the steers quieted. Then the boss and one of the men had seen a light swinging in rapid circles.

Thinking the cook was signaling with a lantern to announce that the belated supper was ready, the boss swore he'd tear the man apart for doing a thing that was apt to scare the daylights out of the steers.

But instead of the cook, he found a frantic settler in white underwear standing just outside a dugout.

"I'm in a hell of a shape," the man said. "Thought it was an earth-quick."

A glance by the lantern light and the boss saw what had happened.

When the steers made their run some of them passed over the dugout, and one dropped through within inches of the bachelor farmer's cot. Snorting and lunging, the wild-eyed steer wrecked the place, and the man thought he was lucky to get out alive. It took an hour to get the steer out of the damaged dugout.

For a couple of nights there was talk around the widely scattered camping area of trouble between two cowboys. At a place like this, with little to do except wait for the reddish flow of the river to narrow, a good fight or maybe a little gunplay would liven things up, and the men around the camps talked of the prospect.

The two principals came together just before dark one evening, and one of them, a slight lad named Burt Phelps, was shot to death. The other one got on his horse and departed. No one knew anything about the dead cowboy except his name. His boss suspected that he was from a well-to-do home in the East and had wandered west for high adventure. The men searched his bedroll and his clothing, but they found nothing to throw light on his background or to indicate where his people lived. In a shirt pocket they found a small soiled Bible. On the flyleaf was written in ink: "From mother to her son."

The little Bible was buried with him there in the valley of Red River.

Other herds drifted in the next day. The first of six outfits belonging to Ellison and Deweese of southern Texas was bossed by Bill Green. Ellison and Deweese had fifteen thousand cattle on the trail—in six herds scattered a few miles apart. Each herd had a boss, a wagon, two yokes of oxen and forty horses.

One of the Ellison and Deweese outfits was bossed by N. P. Ellison. It camped on Panther Creek, a wooded little tributary to the Red. In the afternoon, some of the men spotted a fat yearling that was unbranded. They knocked it in the head, skinned it and took it to camp. The cook stretched a lariat from the front bow of the chuck wagon to a tree, and there he hung the fresh beef.

Coming to the wagon at midnight off third guard, the time when the bedded herds were restless, E. F. Hilliard was startled almost out of his wits. He saw a long, lithe panther crouched on the wagon double-tree looking up at the beef. Impulsively, Hilliard jerked out his .45 pistol and fired.

The air-splitting roar of the gun in the dead of night boomed up and down the river. The other men in the outfit were sleeping some twenty feet away. They came alive, yanked on their pants and headed for the horses. Later, Sam Dunn said the men figured horse thieves or rustlers were raiding the camp.

When E. M. Storey leaped out of his bedroll, he saw a movement at the front of the wagon, but he couldn't see clearly because his eyes weren't accustomed to the dark.

He cocked his pistol.

"What is that?" he shouted. "Speak up or I'll let loose!"

Hilliard spoke up, "A damned panther stealing our meat."

By this time, the herd was on the move. A few hundred of the cattle broke away and ran five miles. This stampede excited all the herds for miles, and the men in all the outfits were in the saddle the rest of the night.

Next morning the cattle in the scattered herd were rounded up. They were bedded that night in the same place, but with more men on guard. The boss stayed awake, with his horse saddled and the reins in his hands.

While circling the herd at two o'clock in the morning, G. W. Mills met another one of the men and they stopped to chat. A bloodcurdling scream rent the still air.

"What—what was that?" Mills asked.

"Panther."

The cattle jumped. The men closed in.

Ellison, the boss, jumped on his horse and rode to the herd. "Sing to 'em, boys!" he shouted. "Sing to 'em."

And the rest of the night the men slowly circled the herd, chanting to the restless cattle.

The next morning the men took a vote on their situation. They decided they would rather swim surging Red River than to camp on Panther Creek with the panthers.

They broke camp and pointed the herd toward the waters of the Red and the Indian country that stretched to the north. By this time the cattle were accustomed to swift water. They had crossed a good many streams on the trail from southern Texas; only recently they had swum the Brazos and the Trinity. So the men didn't have a great deal of difficulty in starting the strung-out herd across the river. Hesitatingly stepping into the water, the cattle raised their tails and heads. When the leaders reached deep water, only a procession of heads and long horns could be seen.

Al McQueen rode into the river alongside the cattle at about the center of the herd. When he reached deep water, his horse, refusing to swim, went into tantrums—rearing, plunging, kicking. McQueen nimbly leaped off the horse onto the back of a wild steer and rode safely across—without losing his hat.

One by one the outfits broke camp, crossed the Red and disappeared into the grassy realm of the Indian nations. But more herds were coming. One of them was bossed by a hard-riding young man who, though in his twenties, had a trail reputation as "a man with hell in his neck." He was Ab Blocker. With him were his brother, Johnnie; a Negro cook, Joe Tashby, and fifteen other men. They had three thousand big steers and were headed for Cheyenne.

The Blocker outfit camped on the Red only one night. They were on a fast schedule—eighty days from the middle of Texas to Cheyenne—and had no time to wait on surging rivers. In later years, when Blocker was an old, old man and honored with the title, "the king of trail drivers," he recalled his trip across northwest Texas that year.

"The cow outfits up there had organized to fight rustlers and to keep their stock from mixing with trail herds," he said. "We heard of this down the trail even before we got to Fort Worth, and we found that these men meant business. It looked like every man had a Winchester and a six-shooter or two. And even the boys were dressed that way. The way I remember it, was that it looked like a place where the kids teethed on .45 caliber cartridges."

Fully as vigilant as the observant drover had been, the cowmen rode their range rounding up their own stock and keeping alert eyes on the herds crossing, and camping in, their territory. Results of the new association's policy of every man a watcher and range police were added up when the cowmen rode back to their "planning oak" in August to sort out problems and fix rules for the fall roundup.

President Carter was enthusiastic. Upon at least three occasions in his district, rustlers had stolen bunches of cattle and attempted to sell them to questionable trail outfits. In each case the boss saw Association members in the vicinity and informed the rustlers of the new deal. The thieves abandoned the cattle, and they were recovered by Association members for their owners.

Others had similar reports from all the six districts. To say the least, the cowmen had made a dint in the dirty work of a range period known as "the years of the big steal." In addition to frightening off rustlers and breaking up sales of stolen stock, the cowmen cut out a good many beeves that had become accidentally mixed with traveling herds. At their August session they could account for at least three hundred cattle that had been recovered.

Kit Carter and Secretary Loving had other good news. The Association was taking hold. A good many cowmen who had scoffed and backed away from the idea of an organization were now joining up, and paying the nominal dues. Things were looking *bueno* again. The range was in excellent condition for the winter. Markets at the end of the trails had been better than in recent seasons; the price of cattle was easing up. With prospects so bright, the cowmen felt good —so good, in fact, that they were generous in special thanks to the folks at Graham who had been their hosts three times that year of 1877 for their meetings under the oak. They passed this gentlemanly resolution:

Whereas, the members of the Association have enjoyed the hospitality of the people of Graham City in general, and the fair ladies in particular, for which they [the cowmen] are profoundly grateful; therefore, be it resolved that the thanks of the Association are hereby tendered to the people of Graham City for their appreciation of our presence in their city, and we indulge the hope that the choicest Blessings of Providence may attend them while sojourning on this range and that in the final roundup they may be received in the Grand Ranch Above.

Firm in the Saddle

BEE HIVE SALOON

Within this hive we are all alive.
Good whiskey makes us funny;
If you are dry, step in and try
The essence of our honey.

This sign, a large one, was nailed up over the door of the
Bee Hive Saloon in Fort Griffin. It was freshly painted and
put up for a particular purpose. The cowmen were coming
to town—for the Association's fall meeting in 1878, the first
convention held outside the shade of that old oak at Graham.

Riding into town, the cowmen saw the Army post high on
a hill. Down on the flat lands at the foot of the slope sprawled
the civilian part of the village which had given birth to big-
time rustling. A good many of the houses were of yellowish
native stone, but there were weathered shacks and a few
tents. Here the visitors noted buffalo men, skinners, bull-
whackers, former soldiers, gamblers, toughs and a few silent
Indians—some of whom were almost certainly rustlers.

Editor Ed Robson of *The Frontier Echo* at Jacksboro attended the meeting. His report indicated he had a high-heeled
good time:

After supper Saturday evening, 17th inst.[November 1878],
we mounted Old Black Joe and accompanied George B. Loving
[a brother of Secretary Jim Loving] to his beautiful home, sev-

69

enteen miles from here, in Lost Valley, where we were hospitably entertained until Monday morning, the 19th inst., when, with that bully-good fellow, Pat Sweney, we lit out for Griffin to attend the semi-annual meeting of the Stock Raisers Association of Northwestern Texas. It is unnecessary to state that our friend, Loving, furnished us horses, buggy and grub for the trip, but such is the fact. We drove late and started early and, of course, on arrival at Griffin, stabled our team with Frank Lampitt and spoiled the looks of the register in the Planter's House—presided over by Mr. and Mrs. Swartz, formerly of this place [Jacksboro] —with our autograph.

After washing the dust out of our eyes, and the "cobwebs" from our throats at J. H. Shansseys, with a hunk of ice, a piece of lemon and "suthin' " else, we were ready for business, but business was not ready for us. . . .

But business there was. Griffin was seething with excitement. People were talking of the lynching—some of them in hushed tones, for in Griffin it wasn't exactly safe to raise a voice against the bloody actions of the Vigilance Committee. In its taming of the frontier the Fort Griffin way, it had handled on a permanent basis eighteen livestock thieves. In keeping its pledge to focus a watchful and righteous eye on the morals of the town, it had strung up a lawyer who had gallantly defended in court a woman who had poisoned her husband.

But the climax hadn't come until sometime before the cowmen rode into town.

A good many persons around Fort Griffin had been missing cows. The animals seemed to disappear into thin air, leaving no tracks.

Even the former sheriff, who operated a slaughter lot in Griffin, said that this outbreak of thievery was the most puzzling he had ever run up against.

One day a cowboy saw a cowhide protruding above the

water in a pond near the former sheriff's lot. It was marked with a brand from a neighboring small ranch. The man who found the hide spread the word, and it wasn't long before the pond was full of men. They fished out a dozen hides with various telltale brands.

Seeing this, the former sheriff took off for some faraway place; he didn't get there. He was arrested and locked in jail at Albany, the county seat.

That night the committee heard that friends of the prisoner, believing him innocent, were about to rescue him. Thereupon, Vigilance members rode headlong into Albany. They stormed the jail and disarmed the jailer. Then they led out the prisoner. A volley of six-gun and rifle fire opened the pearly gates for him.

The cowmen with their rapidly increasing co-operative membership were sitting more firmly in the saddle than the hasty-acting Griffin Vigilance Committee, and under President Carter they cast their influence on the side of law and order. They wanted to round up the big gangs of rustlers, and to do this required range detective work rather than slapdash necktie parties.

President Carter was serving his second term. He had been re-elected the previous March although he had suggested that perhaps a younger man could better serve. Carter's cool-headedness was pleasing to the majority of the members. Serving as first vice-president was J. B. Matthews of Shackelford County, and in the new office of second vice-president created this second year was J. R. Stephens of Clay County. Jim Loving was re-elected secretary and his assistant became George Wright, of Young County. Since the Northwest Texas Cattlemen were attracting so many new members with dues to be paid, the office of treasurer was created and J. A.

McLaran of Palo Pinto County was selected as the first to serve.

Again, as in the previous August, careful plans were made and dates set for the fall roundups. This year the Association took in much new territory, adding three roundup districts and extending its range work deep into western Texas.

By the time of their next meeting, held at Henrietta, near the present town of Wichita Falls, in March of 1879, the cowmen had news of events that made the Fort Griffin episode look like a taffy pull.

The big news concerned John Chisum, the Texan who had trailed his herds to the valley of the Pecos in New Mexico. Plagued by the Indians all the years he had been there and irate because he felt that federal troops were doing little, or

nothing, to protect ranchmen, Chisum had, without the consent of Congress or anybody else, declared his own private war.

He recruited one hundred men and armed them, and they rode with Chisum to a point near the bothersome Indian reservation. There Chisum ordered the men to wait while he galloped alone into the reservation's fort area, his horse burdened with casks of whiskey. He succeeded in getting a good many Army officers tipsy. Then he gave the signal.

His own army dashed in and bore down on the Indians, who were about a mile from the military post. When the smoke and dust cleared, about one hundred and seventy-five Indians lay dead. Never after, it was said, did the Indians drive off another Jinglebob cow.

— HDBugbee

Now Chisum was embroiled in the Lincoln County cattle war, and a slight lad from Brooklyn, Billy the Kid, was shooting on his side. For the safety of his herds, Chisum had driven his cattle into the Texas Panhandle to graze for the duration.

Much closer home, the Texas cowmen decided, like John Chisum, to fight—but by a different method—to protect their cattle.

Their association was still an outfit working with a minimum of cash. For example, at the end of the spring meeting of 1879, Secretary Loving presented this report:

By cash collected in 1878 as dues and fees		$134.00
To postal notices of two meetings in '78	$ 10.00	
To 3 secretary's books @ $2.50	7.50	
To making twelve books of Mks. & brands	30.00	
To postal notices spring meeting '79	5.00	
To Secretary's salary for 1878	50.00	
To balance in hands of Secretary	31.50	
	$134.00	$134.00

So the cattlemen at this meeting in 1879 voted to dig deeper into their pockets and assess themselves any sum necessary to post a reward of fifty dollars for the arrest and conviction of anyone caught stealing a cow from an Association member. A much larger reward, $200, was offered for information leading to the conviction of a horse thief. Horses were, and still are, as necessary as grass and water in the raising of cattle.

Members' sleuthing for each other was succeeding, President Carter said, and dangling gold might encourage ranchers who hadn't joined up with the Association to watch for outlaws more closely themselves. Better yet it might also tempt some rustlers to do a little squealing.

In the free-and-easy days when the ungentle art of mavericking flourished, there was a saying that all a man needed to stock a ranch was a branding iron and nerve enough to use it. Indeed, the influx of settlers after the Civil War included such an assortment of floaters with long ropes and the required nerve that no stray was safe. Therefore, cowmen in the Association took the stand that there were no strays; the unbranded, like the branded, belonged to somebody. The Association declared it was up to the roundup boss, picked by the Association, to determine ownership of strays. In the eyes of these cowmen, mavericking was no longer fair; it would be regarded the same as rustling.

Attention was then turned to the help-yourself custom. If a trail outfit needed red meat to break the monotony of bread and sowbelly, one of the traveling beef salesmen of that day would knock in the head any yearling unfortunate enough to be handy. No one worried about who owned the animal. The owner could do the same thing to some other outfit, and the thought was that sooner or later it would all even out. The trouble was that the Association, located in the big middle of the road, felt that it was permanently on the minus side. Accordingly, the members repealed that unwritten law with this written law of northwestern Texas:

. . . Now and hereafter all stockmen and men in charge of ranches or herds shall kill no cattle or calves to beef except their own or their employer's, and further if any party or parties are found guilty of violating the above they shall pay to the owner double the market value of all cattle so killed and for all calves killed they shall pay to the owner thereof twenty-five dollars, and be subject to prosecution to the full extent of the law.

The cowmen also decided that inefficiency must go, that the practice of "sending a boy to do a man's job" couldn't be tolerated. They approved this edict:

Whereas, there has heretofore existed much confusion at the different roundups brought about by disagreements between outfits sent there; therefore, resolved that each owner of cattle sending an outfit to a roundup, place it in charge of a stockman fully competent to govern the men and avoid all disturbances generally. It is further resolved that each outfit so sent out carry with them ample provisions, cooking utensils and bedding, or funds with which to purchase same.

It was traditional that almost any boy or man could become a cow waddy and pound leather. The cow camp was a good place for a runaway or venturesome boy to land. It was likewise traditional that cowboys, on Saturday night in town, or in towns along or at the end of the Chisholm Trail, would take a drink and maybe shuffle a deck.

The cowmen took a concise shot at this: "Resolved that any employee of any member be fired if caught gambling or drunk."

Moreover, the cowmen, feeling that rustlers or the confederates of thieves might be infiltrating the ranks of ranchers with ulterior motives, decided to check carefully on all men hired to make sure there were no wolves in sheep's clothing. They soon had at hand a rather bulky black list of range workers—men who need not apply for a job with an Association member's outfit.

The black-listed men and their friends didn't like this, and there were signs of retaliation. In the late fall, for instance, when the grass browned and became as inflammable as kerosene, smoke from countless prairie fires darkened the sky. It was possible for a disgruntled man to set whole counties on fire with one match; at least he could blacken untold acres of range.

In petitioning the Texas Legislature for stringent laws against setting fire to grass and woods, the cowmen said: ". . . At the present time thousands of cattle lie dying amid the smoldering dust of our fire-stripped prairie lands . . ."

When the cowmen, in their meetings, passed a resolution it became the law of the Association, and virtually the law of that big region of Texas. Enforcement wasn't as easy as passing a resolution, but there is nothing in the records to indicate that the cowmen ever backed down in their determined efforts to enforce the rules. And they didn't exempt themselves. When a member got out of line, or disregarded Association policy, he found himself subjected to the wrath of his fellows.

With the coming in of settlers and small ranchers arose the contention that these other citizens had as much right to the public domain as the ranchmen. So the cowmen took their stand on this situation:

Resolved that each and every member of this Association respect the accustomed range and ranch of his fellow member, and that any person, whether he be a member of this Association or not, who drives onto the range of any member hereof with the intention of herding or grazing thereon shall be deemed guilty of committing an act of trespass which shall be condemned by each and every member of this Association to the bitter end.

Also that this Association respect the owners of any land in the grazing regions, but that we must strenuously condemn any person or member who shall purchase a small tract of land for the purposes of making a ranch to evade these resolutions and infringe on the range of another.

Resolved that if any person opens a farm within the range of any member of this Association, he will be required to build a lawful fence around the same or must stand the consequences. . . .

Later, with range conflicts mounting, the cowmen laid aside all pretense; they abandoned resolutions and passed a law:

. . . Any member of this Association who shall mark, brand, kill or sell, or in any way appropriate for his own use or benefit, any stock not his own, and without proper authority from the owner, shall be deemed guilty of an offense, and, upon conviction, as hereinafter provided, shall be expelled from the Association.

Any person who shall drive other cattle than his own from their accustomed range, thereby damaging the owner, will be guilty of violating the good intentions of the Association, and on conviction . . . shall be subject to expulsion, suspension or reprehension, as the Association or executive committee, by a majority vote, may see fit. . . . The highest, or first, degree of punishment is expulsion; the second, suspension; the third, reprehension. . . . After a member is expelled he cannot apply for new membership within twelve months. . . . It is further enacted that it is the duty of every member of the Association knowing of a case of branding, killing, driving, milking, or in any way using or appropriating any cattle without proper authority from the owner to report the same to the Association, which binds and obligates itself to prosecute all such offenders to the full extent of the law. . . .

In their early years of battling rustlers and laying down the law on the range, the cowmen faced other issues. Just before Christmas in 1879 President Carter called the ranchmen together to appoint a committee to travel to St. Louis and confer with railroad authorities in an attempt to obtain lower rail rates on cattle shipments. This was the Association's first little round with the railroads, but it was by no means the last.

In 1882, the State of Texas swapped off a province-size chunk of land—three million acres in one patch. Chicago merchants and politicans agreed to build the state a fine capitol at Austin in exchange for the vast acreage which lay up in Goodnight's country along the border of the Territory of New Mexico in northwestern Texas. This tract eventually became the world-famed XIT Ranch, but before there was any suggestion that the land would be developed into a ranch, the Association lifted its voice so that the state could hear:

Whereas, we believe that the sale of state lands in large bodies to one individual or corporation is contrary to the genius of our free institutions and has a tendency to organize and create huge corporations in our state, therefore, be it resolved that it is the sense of this convention that no legislation of any character is necessary for the benefit of the stock interest of northwestern Texas and that we look upon any attempted change of existing laws or the enactment of any new laws on the subject as inimical to the interest of the stockmen of northwestern Texas.

This was a mild complaint—a matter of getting things on the record—compared with the next roar directed at the state and its land policy. From the beginning of the cow business in Texas the grass had been free, the state exacting no charge. But pioneer homesteaders were on the move and they asked their share of the bounty of state lands; their first move was to demand that the ranchers be forced to pay a lease on the grasslands they used. The idea here was to get state revenue from this new source and thereby keep down taxes on other property. The clamor, of course, reached state officials, who even then were warmly interested in the chief sources of voting power, and a lease bill was introduced in the Legislature.

The cowmen started their fight against the lease bill with this expression of opinion:

Whereas, we believe that if the laws now on the books are strictly enforced, the stock interest of Texas will receive that degree of protection and encouragement necessary for the profitable raising of stock. Whereas, we believe the bill known as the Lease Bill, which was introduced in the 17th Legislature, if passed into a law, would be productive of much evil consequence and fruitless of good, therefore we oppose the said Lease Bill. . . .

Fight the bill they did, but to no avail; the era of free grass was soon to end.

The cowmen's troubles were expanding—the rustlers, the settlers, the states and now one of their own breed seemed to be on their heels.

An exchange of letters in the *Fort Griffin Echo* for November 18, 1881, brought into the open the fact that conflict was growing among cowmen and between regions. One of the letters was written by George Reynolds and the other by Goodnight up in the Panhandle.

Earlier in the year, Reynolds had sent a herd northwestward. Before it reached the Goodnight range, the Reynolds trail boss was met by a Goodnight cowboy named Smith.

Smith handed this letter to the trail boss:

George T. Reynolds, Esq.
Dear Sir:
I sent Mr. Smith to turn your cattle so they will not pass through our range. . . . He will show you around and guide you until you strike the head of this stream and then you will have a road. The way he will show you is nearer and there are shorter drives to water than any route you can take.

. . . I hope you will take this advice as yourselves and I have always been good friends, but even friendship will not protect you in the drive through here, and should you attempt to pass through, be kind enough to tell your men what they will have to face as I do not wish to hurt men that do not understand what they will be very sure to meet.

I hope you will not treat this as idle talk, for I mean every word of this, and if you have any feeling for me as a friend or acquaintance, you will not put me to any desperate actions. I will not perhaps see yourself, but take this advice from one that is and always has been your friend.

My cattle are now dying of the fever contracted from cattle driven from Forth Worth; therefore do not have any hope that you can convince me that your cattle will not give mine the fever. This we will not speak of. I simply say to you that you will never pass through here in good health.

Yours truly,

C. Goodnight.

Reynolds had the letter published in *The Echo* along with his own note to the editor:

Herewith I hand you a letter which is so plain that it requires no explanation. I desire its publication that stockmen generally may know how overbearing prosperity can make a man.

Respectfully,

George T. Reynolds.

George Reynolds, whose stature as a cowman was certainly as impressive as that of Colonel Goodnight, was not a man to take a dare or to be stopped by the threat of Winchesters. He sent two herds directly across Goodnight country. One was bossed by his brother, Glen Reynolds, and the other was in charge of Will Howsley. They crossed the plains unmolested by Goodnight riflemen.

Goodnight's dare created enmity of long standing. Reynolds never forgave him. Other cowmen, who found themselves being hemmed in, likewise resented the big plainsman's attitude and vowed to contest his self-assumed right to rule the buffalo plains.

But here again was that old plague—the Texas fever. Not only did herds from lower Texas spread disease and death in other states; they infected the Panhandle. Trail troubles—mainly the result of the fever—were growing by leaps and bounds; even the Chisholm Trail was in danger of being closed. The last safe trail out of Texas to the northern markets ran through the Goodnight country, and Goodnight's letter showed plainly that it was no longer a safe trail.

Only one route looked clear—root, hog, or die, put up or shut up, fight or run.

· 5 ·

The Law of the Range

And there was a strife between the herdmen of Abram's cattle and the herdmen of Lot's cattle: and the Canaanite and the Perizzite dwelled then in the land.

And Abram said unto Lot, Let there be no strife, I pray thee, between me and thee, and between my herdmen and thy herdmen; for we be brethren.

Is not the whole land before thee? separate thyself, I pray thee, from me: if thou wilt take the left hand, then I will go to the right; or if thou depart to the right hand, then I will go to the left.

And Lot lifted up his eyes, and beheld all the plain of Jordan, that it was well watered everywhere, before the Lord destroyed Sodom and Gomorrah, even as the garden of the Lord, like the land of Egypt, as thou comest unto Zoar.

Then Lot chose him all the plain of Jordan; and Lot journeyed east: and they separated themselves the one from the other.

—Genesis 13:7-11.

Up until a few years before the conflict of proximity arose in the West the ranchmen were in about the position of Abram and Lot; they could turn to the right or the left and before them, over the next ridge, river, wood or valley, was more land. They had a horror of being crowded—as did Shanghai Pierce. Shanghai's real given name was the highly appropriate one, Abel. He acquired his more colorful handle his first day in Texas, to which he migrated from Rhode Island. The outfit he wore consisted of such flashy store-bought clothes that the local citizens thought he strongly resembled a Shanghai rooster, known in those parts for its outrageous plumage. Not many moons passed until Shanghai was busy building up an outfit of another color—green grass, blue water and reddish cattle. "I moved," he said, "to get room. Back in the East, when I stretched out to go to sleep one foot would be in Connecticut and the other in Massachusetts."

G. W. Evans, a man of pioneer blood, was another with Shanghai's point of view. "We lived at Lampasas, Texas, my wife and I and two children," he said. "We had a little bunch of cattle and were getting along very well. The country was settling up pretty fast, but I paid very little attention to this.

"Along in the fall of 1883, I killed a nice, fat shoat one day. It weighed about one hundred and seventy-five pounds. I hung it out under a tree near the well to let it dry out good before salting it down. Our house was by the roadside, and neighbors and friends often stopped by to get a drink of water and exchange a few words.

"Several came by that day, and, seeing the shoat hanging there, they would make some remark about it, and, as was the custom, I would invite them to take their knife and cut off a mess of meat and take it home with them.

"When night came, we had only a small piece of one leg of the shoat left. I thought the matter over, and said to my wife, 'This is no place for us. People are getting too thick here and we had better move on west.'

"Right then we began making our preparations to move. John Z. Means was my brother-in-law and when we told him and his wife of our plans, they decided to join us."

The two families loaded up their wagons and headed for the Big Bend country in far southwestern Texas.

"The closest town," Mr. Evans said, "was Fort Davis, about thirty miles away. There was hardly anything there except a few Negro soldiers.

"There were some cattle rustlers in the country, but things were fairly peaceful."

Scarcely twenty years after the cattle business started in Texas and trailed out to the grasslands of the West and the marketplaces to the north, there were no well-watered plains of Jordan left that had not been pre-empted by some Lot.

Cowmen, of yesterday and today, claim that troubles come in herds.

The Winchester-like explosion of Goodnight in the Panhandle was still ringing, with the sounds of all the other little furies, when the northwestern Texas cowmen realized that, despite all their watchfulness and rules, they hadn't begun to whip the rustlers.

In 1883, rustling broke out afresh all over the West; never before in Texas had there been so much thievery—by lone men and gangs who saw a chance to get rich quick. The price of beef cattle was soaring, and there was money to be made.

Every member of the Association lost cattle and when the cowmen got together in Fort Worth for their convention they had blood in their eyes. The first thing they did was to increase the reward for the conviction of a rustler to $250.

Then they took this action:

Whereas, the inspection laws of Texas are inadequate to protect the stock interest, resolved that a committee of five be appointed as a Protective and Detective Committee to hire inspectors to watch all shipping points and feed pens, butcher pens and herds moving out or through the borders of this Association; that the committee have the authority to take over stock belonging to members . . . The committee is further authorized to ask sheriffs of the various counties to deputize the inspectors.

This was it. The cowmen would take the law into their own hands. They would hire their own officers to roam the range and marketplaces, to chase the rustlers down and take them to the courthouse. The cowmen would give themselves the authority to take over stock belonging to members. If the sheriffs wished to do so they could deputize the inspectors, but if the sheriffs didn't co-operate, the inspectors would work just the same.

With this powerful resolution, the cowmen set up a law enforcement body that is unique in America; next to the Canadian Mounties and the Texas Rangers, it is perhaps one of the most famous police forces in the New World.

As we shall see, every day and night since the time of that session in Fort Worth so long ago, the Association's inspectors have been on the range, in the marketplaces and at the shipping points chasing, and catching, cattle rustlers. They have sent thousands of rustlers to prison, and today they are still on the trail of thieves—hotter than ever.

Thus the villain of the range—the rustler—forced the cowmen into tighter organization, and at about the right time. For now virtual civil war broke out in Texas.

"The advent of barbed wire in Texas," W. S. James wrote in *Cowboy Life in Texas*, "brought with it a reign of lawlessness and terror such as has no parallel in the state's eventful history. Then there were decidedly two classes, free-grass and pasture men, and never in any land has there been greater bitterness and eternal hatred than existed between those two factions. . . .

"The first thing that especially aroused the indignation of the stockmen relative to barbed wire was the terrible destruction of stock caused from being torn first on the wire and the screw worm doing the rest. When the first fences were made the cattle, never having had experience with it, would run full tilt right into it, and many of them got badly hurt; and when one got a scratch sufficient to draw blood the worms would take hold of it. Some man would come into a range, where the stock had regular rounds or beaten ways, and fence up several hundred acres right across the range, and thus endanger thousands of cattle and horses."

Barbed wire was a double-sharp weapon in the conflict between cowmen and settlers. In some cases, ranchers used it to protect their range by fencing out settlers, and in other cases the farmers strung it up to fence out ranchers or to isolate waterholes. Nearly everyone cut the other fellow's wire, prowling at night and snipping the tight, bright strands for miles. Any man who strung up wire was in danger; any man who was caught cutting it faced the death penalty unless he was mighty swift on the draw. One of the hardest tasks ever assigned to cowboys was riding along the lines and watching for fence-cutters.

Mainly, the wire was used against the native stockmen. Post by post and strand by strand it was robbing the cowmen of their hard-won bounty which had made the swift rise of the beef cattle business possible—the open range. Cowmen opposed barbed wire at first and fought it because they were convinced in their own minds that they had a right to the range. In a good many instances, the only beings who knew wide stretches of land with placid little lakes had been created were the divine God and the very human cowmen. On this basis arose their conviction that they had a God-given right to the rangelands. But the settlers, being Americans, felt that they were created with an inheritance equal to that of the men who got there first, and they stuck.

Nearly all the stockmen hated barbed wire and opposed it, but finally they came to the hour of decision.

On November 12, 1883, President Kit Carter called the cowmen together at the Association's home office in Jacksboro in an emergency session.

There was to be special action proposed, Carter pointed

— H D Bugbee —

out, but first he had something else to say. He declared bluntly that Texas was in virtual chaos and that the stock interest had to stand up and face the issue. He then introduced a special speaker, Col. Tom Ball, who was to explain the crisis.

"A change in the free range system is inevitable," Ball said, "and the people must accept natural and necessary change."

The booted, big-hatted cowmen were sober-faced and silent.

Ball went on to say that range conditions had *already* changed, that the fencing of small farms and large pastures had come.

He said that the owners of land had the same right to fence for grazing as for agricultural purposes.

In a diplomatic way, he told the cowmen that they could buy land and fence it, that they would have to do this if they wanted range for their cattle.

"The free range is gone," he said calmly, "and the open range is passing swiftly."

No cowman present questioned the logic of Colonel Ball's reasoning. They sat there with their boots crossed and accepted the fact that for the first time since Abram and Lot, free range had vanished and that a new day had dawned, bringing an epoch under which elbowroom couldn't be nudged into but would have to be financed and fenced. No longer were there beckoning frontiers beyond the horizon.

For these cowmen, then, this was the hour of change. Seeing that barbed wire couldn't be whipped, they would live with it. They would be fenced in. They, like Abram, would accede to the choice of others constructively and affirmatively; moreover, they, too, would make the plea, "Let there be no strife."

The following resolutions were adopted:

Resolved, That it is the sense of this meeting that a law ought to be passed by the Legislature that will protect all property rights, either in fences, grasses or houses, with a penalty attached to protect such property rights from wanton and malicious destruction.

That all property taxed by the government is entitled to the same protection, no matter to whom belonging, and whether the property be used for agricultural or grazing purposes.

That it is the desire of this Convention that the people be provided with all necessary public highways or thoroughfares for first-, second- or third-class roads, and that each member of the Association be required to establish gates at all places and points where the neighborhood roads pass through his pasture; and that any member of this association refusing to comply with this resolution be subject to suspension.

"The adoption of these resolutions," wrote James Cox in *The Cattle Industry of Texas and Adjacent Territory, 1895,* "is perhaps the most conclusive answer that can be given to charges that have been made from time to time as to the aggressive and overbearing attitude of cattle feeders and raisers, and their stubborn determination to stand in the way of the inevitable and the impossible. Again and again the public have been told of the monopolies established by so-called cattle barons, of small farmers and ranch owners being crowded out of existence, and of the way in which the rights of the poor have been invaded by the strong arm of the rich. History shows us that in many respects it is the cattlemen who have been encroached upon year after year, and that at least the better element in the trade have invariably opposed monopoly and labored for the common good of the State as well as for the interest of cattle people."

In their quick action, the cowmen prayed the Governor and the State Legislature to stop the cutting of wire and the killing in Texas.

They hammered at this—co-operating with the other cow-men of Texas—until Governor Ireland, in January of 1884, called an emergency session of the Legislature. The resulting laws—those recommended by the stockmen—made wire-cutting a felony, and they also required the frequent spacing of gates in all fences of any length, thus preventing the fencing in or out of anyone. This legislation, enforced by the Texas Rangers, eventually ended the strife, and for a time in Texas it was all right for a man to tote a cocked six-pistol. But if he were caught with wire nippers he was apt to land in jail.

Barbed wire had a partner that received a very different welcome, however, on the plains and hills of Texas—the wind-mill. Its coming brought hope to the land where long wet spells were inevitably followed by long, long dry spells. The clanking, whirling giant with its stream of refreshing, cool water made habitable and profitable, to ranchers and settlers alike, many of the dry, arid spaces that had been avoided pre-viously.

Windmill salesmen followed barbed-wire salesmen, and the shining wheels on the tall stiltlike tower became one of the prettiest sights a tired old boy on the back of a thirsty horse could see as he rode across the range. It was a man-made oasis in all the God-given and, some thought, God-forsaken coun-try. One cowboy who was used to riding herd on cattle down in the south-central part of Texas, where often there was too much water and always too many trees and an overabundance of underbrush, moved out to work on C. C. Slaughter's range, where one dry acre succeeded another dry acre on section after section. About the only growth was the low-growing grass and the weirdly branched mesquite. This boy's job had been to dig mesquite roots for the camp cook's fire and carry him buckets of water from a nearby windmill. One evening after a busy day of digging and toting he formed an opinion:

"This is a helluva country—you dig for wood and climb for water."

At first the windmills followed the railroad tracks, for the puffing iron horses had to have water to run, and the mills were very expensive. Then the railroad started hauling windmills to the Southwest and with the increased volume of sales, the prices went down. Many ranchers and settlers didn't wait on the economics of production. They had a well drilled in a likely spot, sometimes where a willow twig had jerked enough to satisfy the handler that water was near, and then rigged up their own contraption over it. It was reported that a workable mill could be made for $1.50—or less. An example of this type was a windmill made from an old wagon wheel and axle. Boards were nailed on the spokes of the wheel to form sails, and a spike driven into the hub served as a pin for the connecting rod to the pump. The wheel with its axle was nailed up on the top of a tree and with the first puff of wind, the sails went to work and there was the windmill. It was not a thing of beauty, but the water it brought up was as wet as that pumped by the all-steel windmill, "The Aermotor," developed by LaVerne W. Noyes.

Whether the mill was a well-designed model freighted in, or a homemade one, there was magic in the way it produced water. There was tranquillity, too, in its rhythmic pumping that filled the cattle tanks with still waters and, where they ran over, made the pasture grass grow green—a bit of the Twenty-third Psalm exemplified in an arid land.

The sounds of the windmill were not always tranquil, however, for in the winter, when there was a sudden gush of wind, it was the first to announce the approach of a blue-whistling norther. Many ranchers declared they could foretell the weather by the creaking of their windmills in the morning just before getting-up time.

There were still other woes more difficult than lack of water to conquer—the rustler, as ever, and the danger of losing the trails to market.

Kansas stockmen and politicians, who still didn't like the bedeviled bovines of Texas, were getting as headstrong as Colonel Goodnight. Seeing that wire, settlers and other stockmen were closing in on their routes to market, the Texans talked of the possibility of a national cattle highway. Hearing of this, Kansans snorted all over their sun-drenched prairies. No such trail would cross even a corner of the Sunflower State, they vowed. And Kansas took definite action.

The state passed a new quarantine law which permitted out-of-state cattle drives only along the extreme western border. This killed the cattle market at Dodge City as dead as a doornail. No longer, then, could the Texans trail their herds into colorful, violent, salooned old Dodge.

But suddenly, in the midst of these troubles, the cattlemen awoke to the most dazzling silver lining that had ever brightened the clouds over the cow country.

· 6 ·

Riding High

In the early eighties the windows of heaven seemed to open over northwestern Texas and all of the cow country. Except for a Texas dry spell in 1883, rains came at the times of the year they were needed to make the grass green and the watering places fresh, and there was an abundance throughout all the countryside. Land that never before, in the memory of old-timers, had grown sufficient grass for practical grazing was knee-high with succulence. Settlers harvested corn crops that convinced them leaving Iowa was the smartest thing they ever did. Men who had thought raising cattle would be a good way to make a simple living suddenly found themselves rich and the value of their herds increasing every day.

Cowmen of the Northwestern Texas Association had been in the newly blessed country for decades, however, and at their spring meeting in 1884, though their boots were undoubtedly newer than in other years and the strides they took in them were longer, they still had their feet firmly planted on the ground.

The progressive spirit keynoted this March gathering in big Dallas; there was a sense of "Hats off to the new, boys." A respected tradition of the Texas range was done away with, for it had become outdated and made impossible. There would be no more country-wide general roundups. Almost all the range was under fence, and so, when the sage and bluebonnets bloomed from that spring forward, the roundups would be handled by each ranch within the boundaries of its own barbed wire. The new task the ranchers worked on was setting up the range and marketplace detective force so that the ever-roving rustler would find the Association better equipped than before to catch him with any illegally acquired cows or be ready to intercept him when he tried to dispose of stolen stuff. Membership jumped that year, and there was great enthusiasm among the cattlemen for this unique watch on their stock.

The imperative need for Texans to improve the native breed of cattle by introducing new blood was endorsed. E. R. Stiff of Collin County championed the Shorthorns in a much-applauded speech. All sentiment regarding the prolific drought-surviving old monarch of the range, the longhorn, had to be tossed out the window. His flesh was less sought after by Northern and Eastern buyers. The immediate mass improvement in Texas cattle dated from that day. Perhaps as strong as the oratory was the fact that for the first time all the cattlemen, big and little alike, had the wherewithal to buy blooded bulls and high-bred heifers.

With watchful eyes on a fight that was looming if their cattle were to continue plodding inexpensively via the trail to market, the Association membership appointed delegates to a national convention of stockmen to be held at St. Louis in November. The men were instructed carefully to study the plans of the proposed National Cattle Trail and to be ready to battle for it the next fall on the banks of the Mississippi. The delegates were President Carter, Jim Loving, C. C. Slaughter, J. G. Halsell, W. R. Curtis, M. M. Lindsay, Judge J. A. Carroll and many others anxious to make the trip and lend their support if a scrap developed.

Through smoke clouds of hand-rolled cigarettes and fragrant Havana-leafed cigars, after-meal talk turned to prosperity, the greatest this rangeland had ever known, and to the wide expansion and stocking of the West. The figures quoted were large, for the biggest cattlemen in the United States at that time lived in Texas.

Would it be possible, men wondered, for hard times to knock at their doors again—times like those of 1873, when a less savory era of prosperity had ended in panic, and when there was no market for the tens of thousands of longhorns that had plodded to Kansas? Then the price of range beef had dropped to practically nothing. Not until 1877 had it eased up past $2.25 per hundredweight, on foot. By 1882, the price had skyrocketed to $9.00.

A force far from the big pastures had taken hold. Yankee ingenuity, inspired by hard cash rather than the desire to give the lonesome cow-poke something to sing about, surged as only Yankee ingenuity could surge. It had hit upon the idea of the dressed beef industry; rather than hold live animals until they were needed in the slaughter places, the Yankees would dress and store beef; moreover, they would slaughter in the West and Middle West, particularly in places like Chicago, St. Louis and Kansas City, and ship the dressed beef to the large consumers in the East.

Taking another long stride along the financial trail, the Yankees developed refrigeration for railway cars and boats, and they began to export dressed beef. This first refrigeration was known as the Bates Process. In 1875, Timothy C. Eastman of New York City bought the patent and in October of that year he exported his first shipment—36,000 pounds—to England. Within a year, he was shipping three million pounds a month, and then a host of businessmen in Philadelphia and in New York hopped into the new enterprises. By the end of 1881, refrigerated beef was going to England at

The old oak at Graham, Texas, as it appears today. Inset, close-up of marker commemorating the founding in 1877 of the organization which was the genesis of the Texas and Southwestern Cattle Raisers Association.

Founders of the frontier cowmen's organization that became the Texas and Southwestern. Upper left, C. C. Slaughter. Upper right, C. L. (Kit) Carter, first president. Lower left, James C. Loving, first secretary-treasurer.

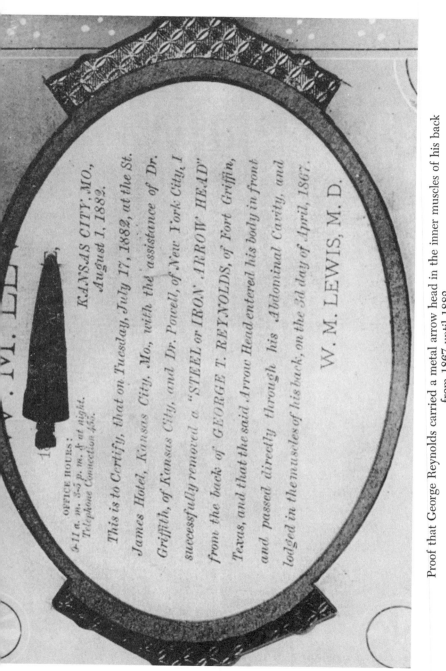

Proof that George Reynolds carried a metal arrow head in the inner muscles of his back from 1867 until 1882.

A longhorn stands defiantly at the edge of a thicket. It was cattle

A Spur Ranch cowboy of close long ago

Dangers of the trail—a herd crosses a swollen river.

Cow outfit. A standard range crew of the 1870's and 1880's consisted of eight men plus a cook and a boss, a wagon, and horses and equipment, including bedrolls, which here are piled high on the wagon.

This cook camped far from shade.
On the range or trail, the chuck wagon was headquarters.

Wagon on the SMS (Swenson) range in the Double Mountain country of western Texas.

Two wagon outfits meet at a watering place near Salt Lake, New Mexico, in 1893. At left (in front of windmill) is the DZ outfit. In front of the house a Curtis Brothers outfit is lined up.

Hauling in 1883. This ox team was driven by J. F. Dennis of Rotan, Texas, (right) and Will Brooks of Snyder, Texas, here shown before the uncompleted courthouse at Albany. The wagons are loaded with wood or cowhides, though buffalo bones—selling for $16 a ton—were a common cargo.

the rate of 110,000,000 pounds a year. This disturbed the British. Beef grazed on the Western range and processed and preserved by these revolutionary methods was selling in England at a lower price than native beef and mutton.

By this time, it seemed as if the Yankees had gone about as far as they could go; but they hadn't. They proved that beef could be safely, profitably, conveniently canned. No puncher spinning imaginative yarns around a flickering campfire on the Old Chisholm could fail to stretch that imagination enough to see how this canning trick could increase the demand for beef steers.

These developments practically repealed the old law of supply and demand. Canned beef would keep indefinitely, and the canners got busy. So the price of beef animals shot upward still more. A man could buy a calf in the morning and sell it in the afternoon for enough profit to pay for his dinner and likely a drink or two. The only way a man could keep from making money in the beef cattle business was to stay out—or to hire out to the other fellow at two tens and a five per month.

However, experienced cowmen, who were conscious of trends, traced the golden flow back to the debacles of 1871 and 1873, when desperate drovers pushed on to lands unknown to them in search of grass and water—to New Mexico, Colorado, Wyoming, Nebraska, the Dakotas, Arizona, Montana, the unsettled parts of western Kansas and the Indian nations. These virgin lands flowered quickly as promising ranch country.

Nearly everyone everywhere hankered for a ranch and cattle and a high-stepping horse to fork, and the range of all the West was claimed, leased, bought or fought over. This skyrocketed the demand for beef animals. Cattle by the millions were desperately needed to stock the new ranges, and up went the prices still more. Texans sold their cattle, especially heifers, for this stocking program, although they knew that they were practically administering a delayed-action sock on their own chins in the form of increased future competition.

Cowmen, new and old, roamed the bayous of Louisiana, the grassy glades of Arkansas and all the South, paying top

prices for native cattle, even runts. The Middle West was skimmed of stocker stuff. In the West, inferior heifers of the sort that usually went to market as culls were kept for breeding cows, and the little bull that traditionally was steered at some roundup camp was now left with his credentials as a herd-sire citizen of the range.

While this new surge of range-stocking was under way and the resultant calves were growing up, there was a scarcity

— H D Bugbee —

of slaughter animals—for current demand, the export trade and the canners—and the price boomed up still more.

Acquisitive men everywhere could smell the invigorating scent of money out West. A. P. Bush, Jr., a native of Alabama and a graduate of the University of Mississippi and the University of Virginia, had run a wholesale grocery business at Mobile, Alabama, and he had then expanded to New Orleans and St. Louis. Now he sold out his groceries and moved to western Texas, where he bought a fair-sized ranch and stocked it generously. Bush, a dashing bachelor, joined the Northwestern Texas Stockmen's Association at its spring meeting in 1884—a tenderfoot who was to become a power in the cattle industry.

Bush was one of legion. Men by the score withdrew money from other investments and plunged it into ranches and cattle. Businessmen and big companies begged for ranches and herds and offered such fantastic prices that some cowmen sold out. Glenn Halsell, long a rancher, sold his herd on the Cimarron in the Indian country to the Wyeth Shoe Company of St. Louis. The company was so anxious to get cattle that it agreed to range delivery—that is, accepting without question the cowman's tally books and not counting the cattle purchased. Halsell's tally books showed fourteen thousand, and the shoe company gladly paid him $340,000.

The call of the West was loud and jingling, tantalizing with the clank of gold and silver dollars as well as the allure of empire, and among those who heard and heeded was Theodore Roosevelt. He deserted New York State and Oyster Bay for North Dakota and a rugged ranch. Frederic Remington, the artist, likewise heard of the land of exciting promise, and in 1883 he moved from New York City to Kansas to labor on a ranch. Another artist, Charles M. Russell, also jour-

neyed westward to absorb the color, throb and romance of
the unparalleled boom.

Men already in the stock business caught the fever, too,
and began to expand, to increase their herds and to seek and
to hold more grassland. Ikard and Harrold, charter members
of the Northwestern Texas Association, bought seventy thousand cattle and drove them to range in Greer County, a virgin
area lying between Texas and Oklahoma and claimed by
both—until in later years Oklahoma finally attached most of
it. C. C. Slaughter expanded into western Texas, buying land
almost by the county until he had a pasture fifty miles wide
and eighty miles long. He also leased a king-sized ranch in
Montana, and he trailed his steers there for finishing. Kit
Carter usually carried around eight thousand head of cattle
on his range; in 1883 he organized the Kit Carter Cattle
Company, which bought forty thousand acres of land and
covered it with fifteen thousand cattle. Snyder Brothers expanded their holdings from the Gulf of Mexico across Texas,
New Mexico, Colorado and Wyoming to the Pacific Slope.

Will and George Reynolds, who had defied the edict of
Goodnight, expanded their Texas ranches and found a new
world of elbowroom in the Dakotas. They trailed thousands
of cattle to this new range. Not only had Texans started the
beef cattle business; they had spread it all over the cow country, and now they themselves were scattered across the rangelands from Mexico to Canada. Early settlers in the Dakotas
and Montana growled that a man couldn't step outside his
homestead cabin and spit without hitting a Texas cowboy.
The Texans were so widely extended that anything that happened to the cattle business, good or bad, affected them at
home and on their far-off range.

M. T. and E. J. Johnson took hold and grew big in New
Mexico and the Indian Territory. Dan and Tom Waggoner

bought more land in Texas and went into the Comanche-Kiowa country north of the Red and leased six hundred thousand acres for their increasing herds. Burk Burnett, the Waggoners' neighbor in Texas and their friend in the Cattle Association, leased range near them in the Indian nation.

Washington didn't want the cowmen in the Indian Territory, but men like the Waggoners and Burk Burnett made their own private treaties with the Indians. Burnett, who had fought Comanches all over northern Texas, was an admiring friend of Quanah Parker, the last great Comanche chief, and Quanah welcomed Burnett and his friends.

Other cowmen from Texas drove their herds into the Cheyenne-Arapahoe Reservation, a grassy empire of four million three hundred thousand acres and three thousand five hundred Indians. Stockmen in southern Kansas likewise needed terrain and they also looked to the Indian nations.

By 1880 the railroad was extended to Caldwell, Kansas, which shot up into a teeming cowtown, and ranchers, headed by Maj. Andrew Drumm, moved into the six-million-acre Cherokee Outlet.

In 1883 they formed the Cherokee Strip Live Stock Association, a corporation to last forty years. Its charter proclaimed its noble purpose:

. . . The improvement of the breed of domestic animals by the importation, grazing, breeding, sale, barter and exchange thereof.

This new outfit leased the Outlet from the Cherokee Nation for five years at $100,000 a year. Men who grazed therein paid two and one-half cents an acre. This raised the lease money and gave the corporation a profit of about $25,000 a year. Barbed wire went up in fences and cross-fences, blocking cattle trails. The incorporators were big stockmen—Major

Drumm (the president), E. W. Payne, C. H. Eldred, Ben Miller, M. H. Bennett, E. M. Hewins, J. W. Hamilton, A. J. Day and S. Tuttle. All lived in the vicinity of Caldwell, Medicine Lodge and Wellington in Kansas except Eldred, whose home was in Carrollton, Illinois. Having leased the Outlet, the cowmen ruled there, and they had absolutely no love for Texas cattle except those from the Panhandle in Goodnight country.

Goodnight found himself crowded. Ranchers stampeded in with their herds, and cattle grazed all over the buffalo plains. All the way southeastward across Texas, Al McFaddin (a future president of the Cattle Association) experimented cautiously with the first Brahmans, the sacred cows of India. Joe D. Jackson, a former Texas Ranger on the frontier, bought cattle and ventured into the wide and wild southwestern corner of Texas which is known as the Big Bend Country. W. B. White and his son, G. R., moved into the Texas hill country around Brady and established an empire. Tom Windham drove his herds from the piny woods of eastern Texas to the mesquite-studded dry prairie of Callahan County in the middle part of the state.

The Scharbauers, who had been sheepmen, started building an empire of Herefords in far West Texas around Midland. L. C. Brite, a cowboy who helped drive a herd from Frio County to the lofty mountains and deep canyons of the Big Bend country, established near the Mexican border what became the famed 128,000-acre Bar Cross domain. In southern Texas, Captain King enlarged his empire by buying land and breeding more cattle, and so did his one-time partner, Mifflin Kennedy.

Prosperous times gave Jim Loving a chance to get back into the cattle business. He stuck to his job as secretary of the Cattle Association and his management of the range police

force, but simultaneously he became a partner in the successful Loving Cattle Company.

There were signs of plenty on the range itself. Ranchers
converted money from the sale of their cattle into building
materials. Substantial homes were erected with enough
rooms, gingerbread grillwork and porticoes to compensate
for the years large families had lived cramped up in log cabins
and dugouts. There were hand-carved stairways and bay windows to delight Western women's hospitality-loving hearts.
Rose gardens were planted to create spots of beauty for fem-
inine eyes that before had watched eagerly for the rose bush
or honeysuckle, brought west as a shoot from Alabama or
Mississippi, to put out growth in the spring. In the kitchen
was a treasured possession—a faucet that brought running
water into the house from the windmill.

Horsehair sofas and pianos adorned the parlors, and fire-
places were designed with artistic mantels. The good taste and
the love of a beautiful home that Texas ranch women had
sublimated while they helped their husbands in this new land
could now be satisfied, and the sky looked to them as if it
were full of lucky stars.

It was while the lucky stars were shining that George
Reynolds decided to leave his range long enough to go to
Kansas City and "waste his money on doctors and hospitals"
having the arrowhead removed from his back.

The British didn't like to be left out of anything that was
flourishing so delightfully. If the beef steer of the American
West was to make the British sheep and ox unprofitable, the
British capitalists wanted in on the financial reward. Moreover, a wide domain of land and cattle had the feel of empire—
something like a rich colonial possession.

So it was that British money, influence and perhaps some

staid culture poured into the Western range enterprise. J. Adair of Ireland financed Goodnight in the Panhandle. British royalty established and ran at a dignified loss the Rocking Chair Ranche on the buffalo plains, and rich Scots in Dundee bought out the big Matador, soon to be run by a man more colorful than the kilts of his native Highlands, Murdo Mackenzie. By 1884, British capitalists and empire-seekers had invested untold millions in rangeland, cattle, horses, chain harness and coats of arms in Texas, Oklahoma, New Mexico, Colorado and Wyoming—much of it in the Texas Panhandle, where the cowboys sometimes referred to the foreigners as "elegants" or "velvet britches."

In tune with the times, the Chicago capitalists, who were building the Texas capitol in exchange for three million Panhandle acres, turned their tremendous terrain into a ranch, and a British company put up the money to stock and run the outfit.

A near neighbor of this tenderfoot in seven-league boots was the 250,000-acre Frying Pan, bought and stocked by Glidden and Sanborn, the barbed-wire kings, to prove beyond doubt that their wire was the very thing the veterinarian ordered. Bates and Beal of Boston founded and stocked the LX Ranch near the present Amarillo.

Thus within a few years, the western part of the United States was populated with cattle and hopeful men on horses. The demand for cows and grass was unlimited, the price high, and never before had there been such a boom in the New World discovered by Columbus.

It was during this time that an unshaven, dust-coated cowman rode into San Antonio straight from his range work one night and tried to register in one of the better hotels. Looking over the prospective customer, the clerk told him he would have to change his attire before giving the hotel the privilege of accommodating him.

"The hell you say!" the cowman stormed. "Why—damn you—I'll build the best hotel in San Antone right across the street and put you out of business."

And—the story says—he did.

The nation had its first full crop of colorful millionaires. At any Western convention a score of men with trimmed beards looked up and answered when someone called out, "Colonel!"

The romance of the long trails, the infinite space and the pastoral picturesqueness of the beef business excited the imagination of the journalists, and for the first time the term "cattle king" came into wide print. Any gentleman appearing in an Eastern city in boots, ten-gallon hat, and flannel shirt and with a cowhead on his belt buckle was apt to be written up as "that well-known cattle king." The term was never popular with the rangemen themselves.

Within a ninety-day period in the summer of 1884, some 825,000 north-bound Texas cattle plodded past a given point in the Indian Territory just north of Red River. During that summer, Ike Pryor trailed fifteen herds of three thousand cattle each to market and sold them at the highest prices ever known up to that time. He put his money in more cattle and extended his operation into Colorado. Pryor, who had started as an orphaned cottonpicker, was offered $700,000 for his herds. He had left his cotton sack far behind.

In these drives, Pryor lost about a thousand cattle, which strayed or became sorefooted and fell out of the herds. Most of these animals became mixed with cattle belonging to others.

"For a year or more," Pryor said, "when I'd be at a convention in Fort Worth, Kansas City or Cheyenne, some man would walk up to me and say, 'Colonel, what was your road brand in '84?' When I'd tell him, he'd pull out his checkbook and say, 'I owe you for three steers that got in with mine.' "

But, even in prosperity, when easy money made the usual headaches less difficult to bear, the stockmen may have felt a few pangs when they saw the easygoing ways of the cow country changing so rapidly. Thomas Sturgis of the Wyoming Stock Growers Association sized it up, "The time has come when our business can no longer be done by the old rule-of-thumb method. In former days we had only to brand our calves when they dropped and ship our beeves when fat. The calf tally could be kept on a shingle, and the checkbook was the only book kept, and the balance or the overdraft at the bank showed the whole of the business. Times have changed."

A sort of cattle aristocracy grew up in the West—not just in Texas, but across the broad country that slopes up the Rockies from the middle of Kansas and down on the other side. If you ran cattle, you "belonged." This was more evident in the newer range country where the operators knew only prosperity and not the bad years of the past as some of the Texans knew them.

The Careys and the Warrens had hurried into wide-open Wyoming, which had as big a cattle boom as any part of the West. Rich men from the East—Philadelphia, Boston, New York—gave Wyoming and Cheyenne something of a dash of culture. As a young man, John M. Kendrick, a Texan, had helped trail a herd of Texas cattle to Wyoming. He liked the highland range, and he stayed. Out there, the Wyoming Stock Growers Association was in the saddle.

In prosperous 1884, the Legislature of the Territory of Wyoming recognized the bylaws and rules of the stockmen's organization and placed control of all roundups in its hands. This meant that the Association was legally in control of the livestock business, and, like the Northwest Texas Association, its laws were hard on rustlers. The law of 1884 defined the maverick or stray and stated that all foremen of roundup districts were to take up mavericks or strays and sell them at auction on the range every ten days while the roundups were in progress. Upon sale of the mavericks the roundup foreman was to brand the animals with the mark of the purchaser and the brand of the Association. Money from these sales went to the Association to hire more inspectors to chase more rustlers. Thus the maverick was now chasing the rustler, a direct reversal of the system of other years.

It was during this time that the historic line of political succession—president of Stock Growers, then Governor, then U. S. Senator—got its start in Wyoming; Francis E. Warren traveled that route, and so did Kendrick; so did Joseph M. Carey and his son, Robert D. Carey.

The rich young men who moved boldly to the wild and woolly took with them some class distinction and certain extravagance. For one thing, they established the plush Cheyenne Club—on the location now occupied by the Cheyenne Chamber of Commerce, which, with undying enthusiasm, keeps the world aware of the Frontier Days celebration out there.

The club was something of an international institution. John Clay, cowman and livestock commission merchant, said, "One could meet men in London, Paris, the Riviera or on the shores of the Pacific who gloried in the fact that they were members of this unique place."

In his engaging story on Wyoming cowboy days, Charles A. Guernsey reported, "During an evening in August '83 the British members of the Cheyenne Club gave a dinner to the American members who happened to be in town, forty-one sitting down. Sixty-six bottles of champagne and twenty bottles of red wine were consumed. There was much singin', speechmakin' and handshakin'."

Behind the bar in this club was an oil copy of Paulius Potter's famous painting, *The Little Bull.* One Saturday night a young rancher, claiming that the picture was a calumny on cattle, pulled out his six-gun and turned loose on it. He didn't hit the bull's eye, but he did put some big caliber holes in the canvas—which is now probably the most famous piece of art in the Wyoming State Museum at Cheyenne.

Phil Dater, a wealthy New Yorker, was president of the club. One of the members was Harry Oelrichs, a brother of Herman Oelrichs, at that time a power in the New York financial world. *The Cheyenne Sun* of November 10, 1883, had this item:

Mr. Harry Oelrichs yesterday received direct from London a splendid English drag. The vehicle was sent to the Cheyenne Carriage Works where it was mounted and where several hundred people inspected it yesterday afternoon. The drag seats twelve persons on top, four inside, and four or six horses are used. The vehicle weighs, box and all, 4,200 pounds, its net weight being something like 3,500 pounds, and it cost something like $4,000. There are but few of these vehicles in the United States, none west of the Mississippi, and the elegant drag will be an interesting spectacle on the streets of the city.

Members of the club sported tuxedos for evening events, and the range-riding cowboys who still pounded leather for less than a round dollar a day referred to these dress togs as "Herefords," proving that the punchers had an imaginative sense of humor if not enough money to get into the exclusive club and dress in starchy white fronts themselves.

Something of a social conscience, with economic tendencies, rose among range cowboys in this time of prosperity. The good times added no money to their pockets, and in scattered places over the rangelands they let it be known that they realized that the stockmen were getting the goody while the cow-pokes were getting the hull.

In the bitter cold January of 1884, the Wyoming Stock Growers Association received a piece of mail worth preserving. It was a penciled sketch showing a corral made of posts bound together with rawhide. Each cowboy in the corral wore a pistol, crook-shanked spurs, leather chaps and broad-brimmed hat. A Texas longhorn cow was shown pawing the dirt. Her brand was the Bridle Bit of Sturgis and Goodsel. The sketch was labeled, "Cowboys holed up for the winter."

The message thereon was:

STOCKHOLDERS PETITION

Hat Creek, Wyo.
March 18, 1884.

We, the undersigned Stockholders in Laramie and adjoining counties, ask of the Wyoming Stock Growers that all members shall furnish men with winter jobs and nothing to do—one first-class Knife to play Mumble-peg with, also Fishhook and Line, three kinds of Pie three times a day, and twelve horses to every man, an extra force of men to do day and night herding. Allow these claims or leave the country.—Long Bill, Old Per Cantuck, Bean Belly, Arkansas Bob, Wild Cat Dick, Bullfrog Bill, Broncho Bill, Big Foot Charley, Blondie Bill, Billy the Goat, Crocodile, Tiny Bill, Sooner Jim, Buck Shot Bill, Windy Bill, Old Fatty, Ragged Bill, Night Hawk, Coyote Bill.

In March of 1883, at the booming cowtown of Tascosa in the Texas Panhandle, two dozen punchers on the LX, LIT and LS ranches, all big outfits, handed their bosses a written ultimatum—higher pay by April 1 or a strike. The ranchers didn't meet the demand and the leather-pounders pulled the first cowland strike in history. They camped at the edge of Tascosa, hoping to halt the spring work and thereby realize their demands. They had a little pile of money to sustain their strike. Girls from the dancehall part of town visited them a time or two, taking along a supply of whiskey for sale. The strike fund was soon exhausted, and before long the men were back in the saddle at their old wages.

It was no trouble to hire cowpunchers. Adventurers were riding in daily, and there was a dribble of settlers who were willing to work for cow outfits at wages even lower than those the cowboys were drawing.

Every sort of cattle rustling flourished, and there were rustlers who long-roped and hot-ironed their way into the cattle business—and on a big scale.

In one respect, the law was on the side of the rustlers. If a suspected thief were caught and taken into court, he was apt to go free and win the congratulations of some of the jurors. It was almost impossible to get a jury of twelve good men that didn't have on its list at least one man who had got his rope on a stray; so there were a host of hung juries.

At one session of the Cattle Association the executive committee reported, somewhat sadly, "A band of thieves have been raiding the ranches in Greer County. We have helped catch some of the thieves. The grand jury has indicted, but these men have not been convicted by juries. . . . Therefore, we must appeal to the United States District Attorney for help in prosecuting thieves in and near the Indian Territory."

However, the rustlers were well aware of the Association inspectors. In 1883, these detectives recovered 501 stolen cattle worth $12,500; in 1884, the catch was 853 head, worth $21,325.

To the northwest Texas cowmen their determined fight against the rustlers was always the most important business on their docket. In the first year of the detective and protective committee, the Association's men inspected a few more than a million cattle. At the marketplaces, 344 stolen or stray animals were recovered; 166 were cut out at shipping points, and 343 were picked up on the trails. This brought the total to 853—worth in excess of $20,000. "There is no way of estimating the number of cattle saved from rustlers," President Carter said. "We are beginning to lock the barn before our stock is stolen."

The glories of prosperity didn't blind the sun-squinted eyes of the Texans to the possibility of great woes, such as losing their trails. The trail-blocking action of the states and territories to the north made brothers of the Texans.

Except for Goodnight in his Panhandle realm and the neighbors he influenced, the Texans were united behind one big idea—a national cattle trail.

And now, late in prosperous 1884, they figured the time was ripe to put up a bold battle for their proposed trail. Instead of oiling their six-guns in the manner of tradition and necessity, they shined their boots, trimmed their whiskers, dusted off their hats and got ready to fight off home ground.

· 7 ·

Roundup in St. Louis

There was an undercurrent of intrigue and excitement that brisk November day the Texans got together in the smoky air of St. Louis. The National Stockmen's Convention—proclaimed as an event that would be devoted to solving all range problems through understanding—was about to start its hopeful sessions.

Meeting in a hotel lobby wildly festooned with horns, hoofs, mounted livestock heads and wagon wheels, dramatically arranged to show off to advantage everything calculated to be dear to the hearts of men of the West, the Texans went over their strategy. They realized that there were differences among them. All Lone Star hands were not outstretched, even so far from home and at such a brotherly gathering. Panhandle men were still ready to shoot if necessary to keep disease-carrying stock from other parts of the state off their range. With that one geographical exception, the Texans were together in trying to work out their mutual problem— getting to market. They hadn't started large-scale shipping by rail, for it was still much more expensive than hitting the trail. But it was obvious that most of the trails soon would be fenced out of existence and on those that remained open their cattle would be most unwelcome; therefore, an official cattle highway available to everyone seemed the only answer. The location of such a route was the stingeroo that put wrinkles in their foreheads.

Capt. Richard King from the great King Ranch empire proposed that all the cowmen organize a company or federation and buy a strip of land for a cattle trail. In this way the stockmen would control it and it would not be subject to periodic political whims. The opposition pooh-poohed the idea, saying, "No, not that. The government should furnish the land, just as it grants big tracts to the railroads." King had to give up, though he knew it was easier and quicker to buy than to beg.

Joseph D. Sayers, a former Texas Governor, was unofficial head of the several delegations. Kit Carter, Jim Loving and Judge J. A. Carroll, famous for his silver-throated oratory, headed up the large northwest Texas group. Captain King, Ike Pryor, John T. Lytle and Shanghai Pierce represented the Southern Texas Live Stock Association. Col. John Simpson, who owned cattle from Texas to Montana, was a delegate from the Texas Live Stock Association, and there from the high plains of Texas was Charles Goodnight, the head of the Panhandle Live Stock Association, which was the youngest and most Winchester-minded of the cattle organizations in Texas.

The Texas rift was not the only one apparent in St. Louis. Two years before, Chicago beef interests, co-operating mainly with northern stockmen, and with Wyoming, had held a national convention in Chicago, and had met again in 1883.

But St. Louis was claiming its session as the first really national convention. Behind it all was the struggle between Chicago and St. Louis for dominance as a livestock market. Chicago claimed that St. Louis had conspired with Southern stockmen in an effort to steal Chicago's thunder. So not only were the two cities fighting; they were splitting stockmen.

Robert D. Hunter, who had been a pioneer on the early trails and had shifted to the more dependably lucrative position of livestock commission man of St. Louis, had conceived the idea of the St. Louis show. He and his associates believed implicitly that St. Louis could wallop Chicago and develop into the great livestock marketing center of the nation. Hunter had sold St. Louis on this key-to-the-city, grand and glorious splurge—one that was to be so spectacular and enthralling that it would wed the cowmen to St. Louis for eternity.

So the big city of the "Show-Me" state decided to show them—it killed the fatted steer. There has never been since an orgy of the splendor, the spending, the show of wealth to equal that of the St. Louis convention.

This splendor was not the idea of the cowmen, and certainly not the weathered veterans who had enjoyed previous booms and suffered as many busts. It was a St. Louis promotion designed to publicize the city. The cowmen and their problems were merely props and headline bait. However, the affair did have appeal on the range, especially among some of the latecomers.

The *nouveaux riches* of the wide prairies, those also new in the cow business gloried in the courting. They had a chance to strut, to drink and to please and parade beautiful women; it gave them an opportunity to stand up and say their piece and to be admired, and perhaps envied, by the multitudes. The old hands enjoyed the fun and frolic, but they were here on business; they were working in the midst of frivolity for tomorrow, since they well remembered some yesterdays.

The spirit of high, wide braggadocio was exemplified in the official band which was led by a high-stepping drum major,

Capt. J. S. Welch. He carried no baton but a pair of highly polished, glistening cow horns measuring five feet from tip to tip. Suspended from the horns was a banner boldly lettered:

COWBOY BAND, DODGE CITY, KANSAS. $20,000,000.

This $20,000,000 figure broadcast the cash worth of the cowmen whose outfits were represented in the band on that golden day of the pre-income tax age.

The cowhand musicians wore blue shirts, leather chaps, boots, spurs and a brace of ivory-handled, hand-carved six-shooters in heavy leather holsters. Their big, white felt hats had leather bands marked with the figure of a snorting steer and the brand of the ranch of which each was the representative.

These boys were from Kansas ranches in the vicinity of Dodge City and Parsons. Unheralded in cow country history except for the few days of glory at the convention, the musicians were J. W. Eastman, director; D. Mathies, James Smith, Roy Drake, W. K. Robertson, W. S. Reamer, George Horder, H. G. Willis, Harry Adams, Frank Cummins, L. A. Louher, Frank Warren, George Meserale, C. M. Beesen, George Ragland, Charles Ottero, C. A. Miller, W. M. Visquesney and Captain Welch.

The Exposition Building, where the convention held its sessions, was lined with flowers, trees, purple sage and objects of prairie beauty. Two huge vases filled with flowers on the rostrum were made of cow horns. So was the official gavel. And there were colorful banners everywhere, bearing the names of the states and territories with citizens in attendance.

This, it turned out, *was* a national event. Delegates came from Connecticut, Maine, Kentucky, Arkansas, Rhode Island, Massachusetts, Texas, Kansas, Indian Territory, Iowa, Illinois,

California, Idaho, Colorado, Wyoming, Wisconsin, New Mexico, Missouri, Pennsylvania, Maryland, New York, Ohio, Oregon, New Hampshire, Utah, Minnesota, Tennessee. Seventy-seven livestock organizations were recognized with official delegates. England's emissary was Capt. Bedford Pim of the Royal Navy, who told the convention:

The great question in England is the food question. To talk of attacking England by invading her shores is foolish. The best way to attack England to advantage is to send out a gunboat to intercept the ship bearing food to England, and the nation is conquered at once. With England and America united we can knock out the world. We will not have to knock them out because we could starve them out without a blow. . . .

The convention had 1,365 certified delegates, and it was estimated that there were a thousand visiting pistols protecting the persons of those owning the bulk of the nation's livestock wealth. The wives and daughters of cowmen, lovely in gowns and jewels planned a whole year in advance, were there, and they wandered in and out of the city shops happily laden with packages.

Governor Crittenden of Missouri and Mayor Ewing of St. Louis opened the convention and introduced a stage load of distinguished guests, including General Sherman. Judging from the applause that exploded when the general was presented, he was more popular in St. Louis than in Georgia or Texas.

The festivities were, of course, a fine picnic for the newsmen. For the first time, the nation and the world got a journalistic view of the rich range business rather than a predominance of stories about the cowboys who rode like Comanches and whirled lariats with the skill of Mexican *vaqueros*.

Later from press reports, James Cox assembled one of the more significant stories of the convention:

. . . The great broad-shouldered, brawny, bearded men, although they looked not quite at home, showed a proud consciousness of being welcome. These were the cattlemen of the West, coming together in St. Louis to their first annual convention. There was an unmistakable class look about them—a class look, too, of which every man in the class may be proud. There was the unfettered carriage of men whose lives had been lived on the great plains, who were accustomed to wide horizons, who were used to the open, wholesome air, to much horseback riding, to much camping out. Even in matters of dress and bearing, the cattlemen are peculiar; they wear wide white hats, long black coats, and, as a rule, long silky beards. The toilet sets off the form well, and no man could help being impressed with it.

The men represent many millions of capital, and the most tremendous new industry of America. They are the men who have put a new value upon the waste lands of the boundless West. Their herds, recalling the pastoral days of the world's history, fatten upon a thousand hills, from the farthest reaches of the Republic in the north to the Rio Grande. They are the latter-day representatives of the patriarchs and they have some of the patriarchal in their bearing and manner. The business which has brought them together has been so thoroughly well advertised that there remains but little to be said about it. They come together to consult on the national needs of an industry that represents more capital than would be required to pay off the national debt. There is legislation needed by Congress and by separate states, which the convention discussed. There were a hundred things done vital to the cattle trade, and through the latter trade to the Western country, which gave the convention a paramount importance.

Maj. C. C. Rainwater, a name the Western cowmen loved, was temporary chairman and handled the preliminaries. Then the convention made John L. Routt of Colorado the permanent chairman. M. N. Curtis of New York was selected as vice-chairman, and A. T. Atwater of St. Louis as secretary.

The first official act was the appointment of a committee to work up a constitution and bylaws for the new organization. By this time, the hall was packed and aflutter.

Then Judge Carroll of Denton, Texas, arose. There were cheers and boos and raps of the horny gavel. Nearly every delegate knew what was coming—the Texas issue.

The Texans were in an odd position. They were not despised as individuals, but collectively they were generally unloved by stockmen from other states. With bulldog determination, the Texans had pioneered and established the beef business in the range states, but now the Texans weren't exactly needed in the industry; they were competitors. Moreover, their cattle carried disease. Could the trail-blazing Texans dominate this first national convention?

Judge Carroll looked squarely into the eyes of some pretty clever politicians out in his audience.

The delegates from the Northwestern states were confident that Kansas would buck Texas on the plan for the national trail; therefore, these Northern delegates went along, saying nothing, figuring that Kansas could handle the trick and they wouldn't have to take sides. Besides, with King's idea of buying a trail eliminated, the only way actually to get a national trail was to have Congress set it up; the convention might, as was the practice of the day, memorialize Congress, but that didn't mean Congressional action.

Judge Carroll made his eloquent speech, ending with a motion that the convention, as its first official act, memorialize Congress to establish a national stock trail, beginning at a point on the Red River and extending in a north-northwestern direction to the Canadian border. Judge Carroll stated bluntly that it was the trail question that had brought the Texans to the convention and that it was the only question the Texans would ask all cattlemen to give their direct attention to. By a lack of forethought, Judge Carroll had said there must be a trail "from the breeding range in Texas to the maturing pastures of the North."

"What do you mean, 'maturing pastures of the North'!" shouted a man named Stewart from Montana, leaping to his feet and waving his hat. "The strip of ground on both sides of the Rocky Mountains to the British possession is a breeding ground for cattle, and I fail to see why government aid should be asked for a trail to enable Texas breeders to get their surplus stock through into the British possessions. Thousands of cattle have been shipped to market from Mon-

tana this year because our ranches were overstocked. I'm willing for any men to bring their cattle into Montana in the good, old-fashioned way, as we did. But I don't want the government spending money on a thing that will overwhelm our state with cattle we don't want."

The debate was on. The Texans kept their heads together, Kit Carter, Jim Loving and Captain King advising Judge Carroll. Goodnight sat close by. He would go with the other Texans—provided the proposed trail didn't cross, or come near, his broad range in the Panhandle.

Texas got a little encouragement from Governor Stone of Colorado, who didn't object to a national cattle trail across

—HDBugbee—

Kansas. However, a delegate named Russell from Kansas hopped up. "A good many men from Kansas have been burned already by the cattle trail from Texas," he said, "and we don't want any more of it. Some of my friends from Texas go so far as to say that there is no such thing as Texas fever, but I know to my sorrow that there is. If this trail was not proposed to go through Kansas, we would not oppose it."

Russell's objection was softened a bit by Martin Culver of Dodge City, who came out in favor of the trail. However, there were a good many delegates who knew that Culver bought cattle in Texas and trailed them to Kansas; therefore, his argument bore little weight with the irate Jayhawkers.

Actually, no one wanted, or needed, the trail except the Texans, and other delegates champed at the bit to get their own pet problems under discussion. But the Texans, with the range full of cattle to be marketed, had no idea of giving up. In years past, Texas drovers had herded their cattle through the Indian nations, into Kansas and into Missouri in the face of hostile men with guns; they had managed against all odds to get their longhorns to market, and the verbal threats in a convention hall impressed them, or frightened them, no more than an afternoon shower in the spring. And so they held the floor and they argued. The Texans finally got a committee appointed and they got a memorial worded and read.

It is doubtful whether a dozen copies of the document now exist. It read:

To the Governors and Legislators of the States of Colorado, Kansas, and Nebraska:

We, the Executive Committee of the National Cattle and Horse Growers' Association, emanating from the first National Convention of Cattlemen of the United States, consisting of one thousand, three hundred delegates, representing almost every section of the Union, which assembled in convention November 17th to 22nd,

1884, in St. Louis, Mo., do hereby present the following memorial and facts, to wit: The first National Convention of Cattlemen did memorialize the Congress of the United States, praying for the establishment of a national highway, or cattle trail, from the Red River of the South to the British line on the North. Now, therefore, realizing that such proposed national cattle trail, or highway, must of necessity traverse the territory embraced within the boundaries of one or more of the states named herein, we do most respectfully ask your honorable bodies, at the earliest practical date, to declare and grant your consent to the establishment by the General Government of said national highway, or cattle trail, within and across the territory embraced within the boundaries of your respective states, it being understood and intended that said highway and cattle trail will be located upon unsettled domain, so far as may be practicable, so as not to in any manner interfere with any habitation or material interest, without first compensating such person or interest within the limits of your respective states.

The convention quickly adopted the resolution, thereby silencing the Texans, who, without Colt revolvers or Winchester rifles, had won the first round. The gun part of the trail deal would come later.

For all practical purposes, the convention was over for the Texans, but they sat through the sessions, listening to the talk which put in sharp focus the magnitude of the booming beef business and its new growing pains.

Half the delegates leaped to their feet, shouting, when the Western delegates—New Mexico, southern Colorado, Arizona, Montana and Wyoming—presented a resolution on the Indians. The preamble said the Indians, with the sanction of the federal government, roamed off their reservations, setting fires and depredating the range. The resolution went on to demand that the government keep the Indians on the reservations.

This brought open charges that the cowmen were starting

a move to take over the Indian lands for themselves; also charges that the cowmen were attempting by fraud to get government permission, by whatever means necessary, to assume the chore of keeping the Indians on the reservations and off the range.

The Westerners came right back with the claim that their plan of action was designed to benefit the Indian as much as the cowman, and someone yelled from the convention floor, "This hurts me worse than it does you, son."

In the audience, sitting stoic and without a change of expression, was Chief Perryman of the Cherokee Nation. With him was D. W. Lippe, treasurer of that nation. Also there was Gen. Preston Porter, a member of the Creek Nation and also an official of the Muskogee and Seminole Live Stock Association.

"I have had my range burned over," declared Delegate Moore of New Mexico. "I have during the past year ridden for three days through fire still burning, which the concurrent testimony of every cowman in my region asserted was the result of either carelessness or the criminal intent of roaming bands of Indians, who were depredating upon those ranges stocked with our cattle. I, therefore, in the interest of the Indians on the one hand, and in the interest of civilization on the other—I will say that wherever in the great march of civilization there is standing in the way any obstruction, whether it be in institutions social, or in institutions of race, those obstacles must be lifted out of the way; civilization has the right-of-way to the centuries that are to come. . . ."

There were blazing, warlike speeches from delegates from Montana and Arizona, all blaming the federal government, claiming that it made the Indian a bad neighbor.

General Porter pointed out that in the Indian Territory (Oklahoma) many cattlemen present grazed their stock on

Indian lands by mutual agreement, that the cowmen were making money and that the Indians were learning to raise cattle and make a living on their own.

The controversy raged for hours and ended in appeasement —a weak resolution memorializing Congress to take better care of the Indians.

The Western men—from out where the federal government owned, and still owns, fifty to sixty per cent of the land —had another hard nut to crack. This was explained by E. Nagel, chairman of the Wyoming delegation, in words approved by Joseph M. Carey, president of Wyoming Stock Growers: "These [government] lands are entirely unfit for cultivation; they are only good for grazing. Now we want Congress to pass such a law as will permit the leasing of the public lands. We hope to have the matter so arranged that the government will lease large blocks of land by district to associations of cattlemen, who will divide it out among themselves, thus preventing any man from fencing off the water. You see, they are not doing anything which would be opposed to the rights of other cattle owners . . . The main point is the leasing of the land for the longest term possible."

When at last the laughs, the gripes and growls were corralled and it was time to shut the gate, the convention honored Colonel Hunter for conceiving and putting over the great show by electing his president of the new national association, and he had his moment of glory. The second annual convention, he announced proudly, would be held in the next November—and again in St. Louis. But there were muttered predictions that, compared with this one, the next meeting would be as dull as the love life of a Dakota steer at Christmas and that the new organization wouldn't breathe past its second convention.

Wyoming snubbed the St. Louis session as a farce. Thomas

Sturgis, a power in Wyoming Stock Growers, was the permanent secretary of the organization backed by windy Chicago, and that group had held its second meeting four days before the St. Louis show. So toward the end, the Wyoming delegation walked out.

The big, noisy hall was tense at times. It was a place where a loud laugh told of an undercurrent of rage: Texas delegates cackled when the chair appointed a man from Brooklyn, New York, to a special subcommittee on branding.

The cowmen, each with his own regional woes, were no closer together than Brooklyn Bridge and Red River.

The convention applied only a thin sugar-coating to bitter pills and solved nothing; it did, however, bring to light sectional differences and it also showed as plainly as a new saddle on a white stud that the nation's stockmen, because of geography, because of live stock diseases, because of money, were not united.

For example, Wyoming figured it would be fine for the federal government to make available public lands for grazing, but considered it bad for the government to furnish land for a cow trail for Texas. On the other hand, Texans, with their own range problems, didn't give a hoot about Wyoming.

One thing the spectacle did do, effectively and completely —it convinced the public that the cowmen were getting as rich as cream a foot thick and to quite some extent on public lands "belonging to us." This planting of a false impression hurt the cowmen perhaps more than any national convention, however successful, could help.

St. Louis had the distinction of organizing the most talked-of stockmen's meeting ever held. Its competitor, Chicago, managed, however, to sound the blues about the time the jaded cowmen were riding home from St. Louis. The

Chicago Board of Trade released a startling report; it said that the Western ranges were badly overstocked, that barbed wire had made little pastures out of big ones and that the mysterious Texas fever was a spreading, plague-like disease.

The price of range cattle dipped sharply but not disastrously, H. L. Goodrich, editor of *The Daily Drover's Journal* in Chicago, got off perhaps the most prophetic pun known to the cattle world. After commenting on the dire predictions of the Board of Trade, he quipped, "If you have any steers to shed, prepare to shed them now."

But the cowmen who had been to the big city from Texas, the Indian country and Kansas had too many present headaches to worry about newspaper predictions. It wasn't long after the glitter of the roundup in St. Louis faded that guns glinted in the sunshine out West.

· 8 ·

Come Hell or High Water

On an afternoon in the late spring of 1885 a herd of Texas steers grazed slowly across the Neutral Strip of Oklahoma. The green-carpeted prairie was dotted with blowing wild daisies and buttercups. The herd ambled along, the steers with their horned heads down, their frothy muzzles in the greening grass. The cowboys rode slowly, stopping occasionally to roll cigarettes.

The chuck wagon, tugged by four lop-eared mules, rattled and shook, followed by the horse herd. It was a pleasant, peaceful scene, a much wider pastoral sweep than the decorators at St. Louis had been able to create. This trail outfit looked like the thousands of others that had made the overland journey from Texas to the north.

At the Kansas border a dozen mounted men dashed up, yelling and waving pistols and rifles whose barrels flashed in the sun of the Sunflower State. They rode straight to the trail boss and informed him that he couldn't cross into Kansas, that he would find himself in a damp and remote recess of a Kansas jailhouse if he didn't behave and obey quarantine. Quarantine meant no Texas cattle on Kansas soil.

The steers belonged to Martin Culver, a Kansan, but that made no difference to the grim-faced guards.

The stubble-chinned trail boss sat on his horse frowning at the wide prairie and the milling steers. He motioned his men to him, and when they jerked their horses to a stop in a semicircle, he said, "Bend 'em to the west, men. Nothing in Kansas, anyhow, except the three suns—sunflowers, sunshine, and sons-of-bitches."

That was the temper of the times.

The Culver herd bent westward and eventually grazed northward along the eastern edge of Colorado, just outside Kansas. Far behind this herd, down in southern Texas, a million cattle were mooing out of the roundups ready for market, and there was no trail.

With factions of cowmen from the Rio Grande to the top of Dakota battling with resolutions, politics and threats—to protect themselves from each other—the northwestern Texas ranchers got their heads together in their spring convention of 1885 and did a surprising thing. They passed a resolution expressing deepest sympathy for the employees and laborers of the Missouri Pacific Railroad, which was torn by a strike. This was one of the first rail strikes affecting Texas, and the wives and children of many of the strikers were hungry and sick.

Although they had a sagging market and their trail troubles, the cowmen were broadening their range of view—looking closely at all the facets of the national economy rather than restricting themselves to the cow pasture and the waterhole. Moreover, only the cattle trails were denying the expanding railroads the business of transporting live beef. Texans might need those railroads some day.

A note of sadness prevailed at this convention. Kit Carter, so long the president of the Association, was ill and unable to attend. The strenuous year—the trip to St. Louis and the trail fight—had been hard on the aging cowman. C. C. Slaughter presided at the session, relying on Jim Loving, who was still the secretary and now receiving a salary of $300 a year. Slaughter was elected president.

Having expressed themselves on the plight of the railroad strikers, the cowmen plunged into the fight for what had been the heartbeat of their business. They petitioned the State Legislature and their congressmen to get into the battle to keep the cow trails open. The odds lay heavily against the Texans.

The State of Kansas had decided that the Texas cattle drives had been a plague long enough. Early in 1885, that state had passed the quarantine law the armed men on the border had quoted to Culver's trail boss, prohibiting the moving of cattle through any part of Kansas from most of Texas, lower Arkansas, Louisiana and Mississippi during the traditional marketing season—the only time of year there was reason to drive southern cattle into Kansas, anyway. Almost immediately, Colorado, Wyoming, Nebraska and New Mexico slapped on quarantines that banned Texas cattle, and live stock associations in those states passed bristling resolutions against any visitation of Texas herds.

At this same time, a company which claimed to be in the cattle business leased the Cheyenne-Arapahoe Lands, which butted against the eastern border of the Texas Panhandle. The men who leased the area speedily strung a fence around it, thereby blocking cattle trails that had been used by countless herds since the time of the Civil War. However, they subleased, and cows continued to graze on the reservations.

This swift action blocked nearly all of Texas from market. Then everybody started blaming everybody else. *The Trinidad* (Colorado) *News* led off by wondering about the fencing of the Cheyenne-Arapahoe Lands. It said, editorially:

That was a smart scheme of a railroad corporation which resulted in the closing of the great cattle trails over which the thousands of cattle were annually driven north. A company which had no other capital than gall leased a strip of the Indian Territory for grazing purposes for five years. It had no intention of stocking the range and had no means to stock with. It then took steps to prevent the cattle being driven over the leased lands, which would result in requiring the Texas cattle growers to ship by rail.

One thing the sympathetic editorial didn't mention was the fact that Colorado felt strongly that the Texans ought to have a trail—as long as it ran across Oklahoma and not Colorado.

Not only did the neighboring states and the leaseholders of Cheyenne-Arapahoe Lands knock Texas in the head; Goodnight and the other big cattlemen who had joined him on the buffalo plains of the Lone Star tightened their own quarantine line and manned it with more Winchesters.

However, the cowmen north of the Red, including Colonel Goodnight and his Panhandle pals, didn't clamp on the ban solely because of the Texas disease danger. They frankly mentioned other reasons: The other Texas cattle were competition for their stock and consumed all their grass; also southern cattle tended to lower the grade of their herds because "Texas bulls wandered and intermingled with northern cows."

Despite the honesty of the reasons for the ban, Texans with a million cattle ready for market couldn't stand around with their hands in their empty pockets. They were, therefore, determined to move the cattle northward, come hell or high water.

For the Texans, the issue was as clear as a July day on the Rio Grande; they needed a trail and intended to have one. And so they took up the fight where the St. Louis convention left off—that is, for a national cattle highway from Red River

to the Canadian border. The St. Louis convention had grudgingly appointed a committee of nine men to see what could
be done about the proposed national trail. Texas members of
this committee were Henry Warren and U. Upson, who belonged to the Texas Live Stock Association. The committee
had camped on the Potomac for a month but had found that
only Texans were at white heat over the trail proposal. However, the committee had drawn up a report which emphasized
the importance of getting Texas herds to market in 1885.
Pointing out that any Congressional action would be too late
for the coming market season, the committee asked the
Northern states to permit establishment of an unofficial trail,
on an emergency basis. The committee pledged that southern
Texas cowmen, as individuals and as members of the several
associations, would hew to the line, stick to the trail and prevent their cattle from coming in contact with any herds along
the line.

This trail as visualized by the committee of nine was a
dandy. It would angle across the Neutral Strip of Oklahoma
and hit the southern boundary of Colorado. From there
northward to the Canadian border, it would be 690 miles
long and not more than six miles wide. The area of the trail—
all of it government land—would be 1,324,800 acres. The
land itself, surveying, and the construction of artesian wells
along the way and bridges over the wildest rivers would cost
a million dollars. The committee took pains to point out that
the long, grassy corridor would contain only 2.78 per cent of
the amount of land the government had granted Western
railroads.

Now all the Texas cowmen, except those in the Panhandle,
joined in the fight for this trail, resorting first to political action. The Panhandle men, seeing the trend of the times, allied
themselves with Northern groups opposing the trail; they

MAP SHOWING THE PROPOSED NATIONAL CATTLE TRAIL

likewise resorted first to political pressure. So, in reality, there raged a range war without guns.

Yielding to the pressure of the Texans, Congressman James F. Miller of Galveston introduced in the House of Representatives a bill which would authorize the Secretary of the Interior to appoint three commissioners to lay out and establish the national trail. Senator Richard Coke of Texas introduced a companion measure in the Senate. The Texas Legislature quickly adopted a resolution urging all senators and representatives in Washington to support the trail proposals—and to make it pronto, boys!

Then one day the Texans found themselves totally red-faced. From north of Red River came this suggestion: "The Texans are ranting for a trail to the British possessions across the land of other states, but Texans are not making any effort to establish a trail across Texas."

The thing that hurt was that this was the awful truth. State Representative J. N. Browning of a Panhandle district, who had been a trail driver before the days of control by quarantine, quickly introduced a bill calling for a Texas trail extending from the central part of the state to the Neutral Strip of Oklahoma. It was to be from one to two miles wide and clearly marked with cedar posts, each post branded: TEXAS CATTLE TRAIL.

There were a good many voting Texans—farmers and railroad people—who didn't give a continental whether there was a cattle trail. To say the least, the members of the Legislature didn't get steamed up over the proposal, and the bill was never called up for passage. The failure of Texans to provide a cattle highway within their own state was ammunition for the big guns the states to the north had drawn on Texas.

At this unhappy time a mild reason for hope developed in Washington.

On February 17, 1885, the House of Representatives approved a resolution asking the Secretary of the Treasury to get together pertinent information on the range cattle trail in the Western states, the report to be used in any consideration of the national trail proposal. Joe Nimmo, chief of the Bureau of Statistics, had been primed and was ready for this. Within a short time he submitted a sixty-thousand-word report, with index and appendix, the latter an exposition of the great need for a cattle highway.

With this report favoring the trail and a trail bill pending in each house of Congress, the Northern cowmen began to stiffen their opposition. Governor John Martin of Kansas told his Legislature that he was getting protests against the trail from all parts of the state, and he said, "It is of the highest importance that the driving of these animals through any portion of Kansas during the months when they are likely to communicate splenic (Texas) fever should be absolutely prohibited."

Then State Senator E. M. Hewins, himself a rancher in Chautauqua County, Kansas, came up with a states'-right idea that made Kansas forever oppose the trail. He said, "This trail would remove all embargo at all times on Texas cattle, no matter what their condition may be. This proposed trail of six miles wide would be beyond state jurisdiction, and by means of the Santa Fe and Union Pacific Railways, there would be a means of evading all state quarantine or other laws, as shipping would be done within the six-mile limits."

This startling revelation crackled all over Kansas—the proposed trail would be a federal corridor, and Kansas would have nothing to say about anything that happened in that narrow strip across the western part of the state! Now Kansas really memorialized Congress to junk the trail proposals.

The strong opposition in Kansas stimulated deep concern

in other states. If Kansas, with its laws and its armed guards, blocked the trail, would the market-hungry Texans try to break through elsewhere? This question had a historic answer: in earlier years, Texans had driven their longhorns where they pleased and had bulldozed or outwitted all opposition.

Therefore, the Cattle Growers' Association of Bent County in Colorado was not surprised at rumors that the Texans intended to use that region as a gateway to the north. The members pledged themselves to use all civil means to prevent the establishment of a trail across their country and also to block any movement of Texas cattle in their direction. They ended their declaration by saying that if they were forced to go beyond civil measures, the cowmen in the association would act as a unit.

The Texas Panhandle cowmen joined Bent County and stockmen from the Cherokee Outlet in Oklahoma in a joint meeting at the St. James Hotel in Kansas City. They reported that the strange Texas cattle disease had cost the Panhandle $300,000 worth of cattle. Bent County men claimed a loss of half a million dollars, and Kansas and the Indian Territory placed their losses of the past season at more than $300,000. And they took their stand:

While deprecating the use of force, self-preservation is the first law of nature; therefore, be it resolved that we, the undersigned combined associations, acting as a unit in committee assembled, do hereby pledge our respective associations to resist by all legal and *necessary* means the encroachment of such cattle upon our range.

News of this uncompromising opposition reached the ears of the Texans at a time when all political plans collapsed. Not only did the Texas Legislature fail to pass the Texas trail proposal, but Congress adjourned without getting around to the national trail. Blocked in every direction they had tried to turn, the Texans were angry now, ready to take any action necessary. Rumors rippled over Texas, the most exciting one being that cowmen were buckling on pistols and equipping every cowboy with a Winchester rifle. They intended, the grapevine had it, to shoot their way to market if they couldn't get there any other way.

This tale was given credence when Governor Ireland made an unqualified statement that he could provide Texas with a trail. The remark could mean only one thing—that the Governor had Texas Rangers and their expert marksmanship in mind. With a few Rangers, Ireland could certainly open a cattle trail over state land through the Panhandle—all the way to the Neutral Strip in Oklahoma. From there on, federally owned land extended northward all the way to Canada. The drovers could fight their way over this government terrain, defying the states if the drovers had enough guns to impress the guards, who were also armed. There were rumors that Rangers, assuming the role of cowboys, could ride along with the herds and be ready to take part in any other activities that might develop on the trail.

Amid the talk of the establishment of a trail by force of arms, the Texans lost a friend and a wise, old head. On April 14, 1885, while visiting in San Antonio and staying at the old Menger Hotel across the alley from the Alamo, Capt. Richard King died. Thus the man who had conceived the idea of a trail and who had with foresight beseeched cowmen to get together and buy the necessary strip of land was removed from the struggle at its most critical hour.

R. J. Kleberg, Sr., a San Antonio lawyer who was engaged to Captain King's daughter, Alice, handled the legal details of settling the large estate. When he handed Mrs. King a bill for his work, it read, "$32."

Mrs. King immediately made Kleberg manager of the ranch. He married Alice King the next year.

One of Kleberg's first major tasks was that of getting the cattle to market, and that brought him into the company of the other ranchers—there was no trail.

With tension gripping the length and breadth of the range country, John N. Simpson, president of the Texas Live Stock Association, called on Texas cowmen to meet in Dallas on May 15, and a good many of them came equipped with chips on their shoulders. They were tired of nothing but talk about trails; they were ready to start out with their cattle and fight their way through.

"We've been fenced in, but by damn, we'll not be bottled up," exploded a man from Palo Pinto County.

The Panhandle cowmen, headed by W. A. Towers, were there in full force, and also full of strong arguments against any angling across their country. However, W. H. King, the adjutant general, in command of the Ranger force, was on hand, his presence being evidence that the Governor was still in the mood to blast out a cattle trail, and this stood as a sort of unspoken leavening for the Panhandle men who had the temerity to presume to block a trail across a part of sovereign Texas. Ill tempers and impatience abounded. Simpson, Slaughter and other heads from the various cattlemen's associations kept the meeting businesslike, and finally it was agreed that five men from the northern part of Texas and the same number from the south would labor as a conference committee to recommend a trail route across Texas.

This committee plotted a path slanting across the state to the famed Doan's Store on Red River and then edging the Texas line to the northern end of the Panhandle; then westward across the northern end of the Panhandle to Buffalo Springs, where the big XIT ranch was beginning operations.

From there it would cut across the Neutral Strip and hit the corner of Colorado. After some bickering, the cowmen adopted this trail proposal, which was a compromise: the Panhandle men gave in and voted grudgingly to let it skirt their country, and the southern men agreed on the route, though it was much longer than one straight across the Panhandle.

Of course, the Texans could establish such a trail only to the borders of their state; from there on, other states were involved. But seeing that the Texans were ready to move and taking note of the fact that their proposed route didn't get into Kansas, members of the Western Kansas Cattle Growers Association got together on May 29, and approved the trail; they took this action largely because a good many of the members had cattle in the Neutral Strip. On the heels of the Kansas approval, the stockmen in the Strip decided that they preferred a designated trail to indiscriminate driving over their range, and they approved the route adopted at Dallas. Colorado kept quiet.

Then it was that the Martin Culver herd headed northwestward over this trail. When the Kansas guards forced the boss to bend his herd west, Culver hurried to Washington and got permission to trail cattle along a narrow strip of the extreme eastern edge of Colorado—on federal land, of course, and not touching Kansas, of course.

And, at last, there actually was a cattle route, which was known as the National Cattle Trail, but animosity lingered around many of its endless curves, marked not with strong fences, but only by impermanent, bleaching buffalo skulls.

Forty Million Cloven Hoofs

Kansas and Cherokee Outlet stockmen were wise to the ways of the West, and they knew it would take more than gaunt-eyed buffalo skulls along the National Cattle Trail to keep Texans from using handy short cuts. Accordingly they fortified the markers with well-hardwared guards "to assist any lost drover who might get off the National Trail."

Late in the spring of 1885, John R. Blocker put twenty-five thousand steers on the trail in nine herds that were strung out from below the Alamo to the very top of Texas. George West likewise had several herds moving across the state.

One Blocker herd and one belonging to West grazed into the vicinity of Fort Camp Supply in the Cherokee Strip at the same time. The Blocker and West bosses talked things over and decided they could make time by cutting across Kansas, leaving the National Trail to go its own merry way. They broke camp and started to drift northwestward. Immediately fourteen horsemen came pounding over a row of low hills. They quickly surrounded the foremen, who were out in front of the herds leading the way, and told them the cattle were to stop right there in their tracks—that they wouldn't even be permitted now to go on following the National Trail since it was evident they didn't mean to stick to it.

The bosses identified themselves as drivers for Blocker and

West, but the guards were not impressed in the least. There was nothing the trail bosses could do but notify their employers of their predicament. The two cowmen hurried to Fort Camp Supply. They were in an ugly mood.

Many an armed man had trembled at the wrath of Blocker and West—perhaps the toughest and most determined men ever to look down the bony back of a longhorn. As a drover, West was known as one of the old blue hen's chickens, and it was said of him that he would fight a cyclone with a knitting needle. He was the man who really established trail driving and proved that Texas cows could hoof it almost any distance. Back in 1867, before the trails were well established, West had delivered one herd of fourteen thousand to the Rosebud Indian Reservation just one hundred miles south of the Canadian border, driving them from southern Texas. No other drover ever equaled that trail performance.

Blocker, said by friends to be as stubborn as a blue-eyed burro, had almost as great distinction as a man of the trail as West. He, with his brothers, W. R. and Ab, had driven more Texas cattle to market than any other man. In a single year, the Blockers had taken eighty-two thousand cattle over the Chisholm.

West and Blocker believed in the pioneer ranchman's code, "take a heap of abuse before you kill a man," but this time they really fumed, allowing that the heap was about sufficient. The guards ignored them.

Other herds, following the National, stacked up in the area, virtually blocking the trail. One of the drovers, a friend of Blocker, joined in the fuss. "If you'll give the word, Johnnie," he said, "I'll take my men and kill every one of these fellers."

Blocker said he believed he had the law on his side, and he was going to prove it. He and West telegraphed Washington, keeping the wires hot with pleas to senators and the War Department for troops to escort their herds.

They drafted one exceptionally long message, and the toll ran up to a few cents over $60.

"Ain't this a hell of a note!" Blocker growled, peeling off bills to pay the charge. "Imagine us spending our time and money sending telegrams to Washington when we know how to move cows!"

When the word that Blocker and West were getting ready to shoot their way out of the blockade had circulated sufficiently, a small troop of cavalry was hurried to the scene. Soldiers escorted the herds and they stuck to the designated trail to the inch.

The Kansans thus won the first skirmish, but in the following weeks the Texans grew too numerous and their momentum too great for the border guards. Cattle from the fever country broke trail and went over into the Outlet, into Kansas and into the realm of the Bent County Stock Growers Association in Colorado.

The office of Governor Martin of Kansas was flooded with rumors that a wholesale invasion was being made on Kansas by diseased cattle. Some few of the trail bosses truly didn't know of the National Trail—they didn't read newspapers or attend cowmen's meetings—but many of the drovers were old dogs who refused to learn new tricks; they were just following the stars and heading straight to where they wanted to go. So many herds strayed from the designated route that before the season was over the Trail had proved to be a farce.

The Pueblo (Colorado) *Chieftain* growled:

> Many of the drovers are not satisfied with the one [trail] chosen, and say they "have as much right to drive on the public domain as any cowman has to feed on it," and with some very emphatic blank-blanks they swear they will drive on it, and that no convention shall say what they shall or shall not do. On the other side, all the cowmen not on the trail say that they must stick to that, and a good many on the trail say they can't come there; that they have nine points of the law, and have got guns and "sand" enough to keep them. Further up this way, Kansas, Colorado and New Mexico cowmen are holding the fort with Winchester guns and a liberal supply of ammunition, and a perfect willingness to use it in defense of their range possessions.
>
> The Northern cowmen are tired of having the fever spread among their cattle, as well as having their grass eaten by the through herds. This is the whole cause of the trouble. It is possible it may be settled without bloodshed, but it does not now seem probable. Cowmen and cowboys are pretty ugly customers with a gun, and they generally mean business when they talk shoot. . . .

The Texans, even those who departed from the bison-bone boundaries of the trail, were also talking shoot, and they kept moving cattle. One old Texan, reporting on the year's drive, commented, "We placed our faith in God, a six-shooter and the chuck wagon, and we trailed cattle to market."

The Chieftain's forecast of bloodletting might have become fact had it not been for an ironclad order of President Grover Cleveland on a closely allied matter, which upset the range country and diverted attention. In July of 1885, the President signed an executive directive which gave cattlemen forty days to remove all their stock from the Cheyenne-Arapahoe Land. Cleveland claimed that the operations of the stockmen were irritating the Indians.

Thinking the time limit extremely short, several cowmen journeyed to Washington to demand a reasonable extension of time, claiming that it would be impossible to move the herds within forty days. They had no trouble in getting into the White House, and there they found a genial great white father, but a tough one.

He listened attentively for a little while and then said, "No argument will induce me to change what has been done."

Apparently he had a great deal of confidence in the ability of these booted men to round up and drive cattle.

Within a couple of days, chuck wagons rumbled out in a great procession on the reservation. Smoke and dust spiraled up from innumerable cow camps. Cows with big, frisky calves at their sides bawled and milled. Cowhands rode on four- or six-hour shifts and the work didn't slow down except when it was too dark for a man to see a spotted cow. On moonlight nights the men stayed in their saddles and kept the cattle moving.

The Halsells were among the main operators on the reservation from the Northwest Texas Association. They and their neighbors threw together a herd of ten thousand cows, bulls, steers and calves and pointed toward the Cimarron. Early in the morning the chuck wagons crossed the river, rolled on a mile or so and made camp. The cooks started cooking.

At nine o'clock in the morning the first cows plunged into the Cimarron, followed by the herd that stretched and humped over the hills like an endless serpent. The first men over rode to the chuck wagons, ate and mounted fresh horses and loped back to the work. At three o'clock in the afternoon the last of the great herd came dripping from the river. By that time all the men had eaten and were on fresh horses.

And then one of the range country's biggest cutting, or separating, jobs took place. The several owners cut their own stock from the herd and headed out of Oklahoma. Before dark, the cutting job was complete.

That night in camp, H. H. Halsell heard one young cowboy from a Texas village that was strong on church-going ask another if he thought working all day Sunday was pleasing to the Lord. The puncher replied, "I don't know that I understand it as you may, but I am working for my boss. I guess if I keep the fences up good, and the cattle in the pasture and varmints out and see that the cattle get plenty of water and grass and see that wolves don't get the calves—well, I figure I hold my job. But if I set around headquarters and sing to the boss, I'll get fired."

The dust of the last herd to depart from the Cheyenne-Arapahoe Lands settled and the range was unirritatingly quiet for the red men before the end of the forty-day deadline. A record, with the exception of Noah's, had been set for cattle movement that has yet to be equaled.

Commenting on this historic exodus, *The Kansas City Live Stock Record* twitted: "Perhaps their [the cowmen's] compliance was accelerated by the presence of General Miles and his troops at Fort Reno, with orders to enforce the proclamation."

Cleveland's giving the land back to the Indians, coming at the critical time it did, made cattlemen as nervous as a steer at midnight. Cattle prices had been on a downward trend since the time of the gay convention in St. Louis, as Chicago had warned, and drought was beginning to creep over western Texas. A good many of the ranchers had taken their herds to northern pastures because of this dry spell. Good ranges were crowded, yet the tens of thousands of cattle forced off the reservation had to go somewhere, and there was a frenzied rush to lease pasture. This cow stuff was practically all in breeding herds and not intended, or ready, for slaughter, but men who could find no grass had to rush to a market that was already weakening.

However, the President's action had been cause for some hope; it took stress off the cattle trail. Since there was nothing in the Presidential proclamation to indicate that the use of his cleared-out strip of Indian reservation in western Oklahoma as a cattle trail would disturb the Indians, it was easy for a cowman to interpret this as meaning that it was all right to take a chance on driving across that country. But again there was a complication—specifically, the agitation for opening vast portions of Oklahoma to white settlement. Of course, that would prove a mighty blow to many cowmen in Texas and in some of the states to the north, particularly Kansas. The Indian lands had been used as a sort of reserve empire of grass.

After a huddle on the question the northwest Texas cowmen announced, "Opening Oklahoma to settlement would violate sacred treaties with the Indians."

They ended the resolution with the declaration that depression had hit the beef cattle industry and that the opening of Oklahoma would make it worse.

In these days there were men so wrapped in tradition that they couldn't imagine the cattle business without trails and boom towns and all the color and excitement that had marked the pioneering era. One of them was Martin Culver. At about the time the President ordered the cowmen out of the Cheyenne-Arapahoe Nation, Culver laid out a town on the so-called National Trail—on the shore of the Arkansas River where the Santa Fe Railroad crossed the cattle trail. His town would be barely inside Colorado, so close to the line that a drunk who stumbled out the back door of a saloon would be in Kansas and, therefore, safe from Colorado officers. The cattle trail would be the main street of Trail City.

What Culver had in mind was a new town that would be a reincarnation of the "boomers," Abilene and Dodge, and thrive as they had before dying of "quarantine fever." H. P. Myton, an official of the U. S. Land Office, and W. S. Smith, a land agent of Garden City, Kansas, went into the project with him. They incorporated their town with two hundred shares of stock having a par value of $100 each. By August of 1885, the hammers and saws were ringing in Trail City, and at about that time, *The Pueblo Chieftain* carried a story to the effect that a good many buildings, stores, saloons and a spacious boardinghouse were almost completed and that around one hundred lots had been sold for an average of $150 each.

Saloonkeepers and others who had run business establishments in Dodge and Newton moved over to Trail, which was wide-open in every respect. Any cowpuncher with money could satisfy every need and desire in Trail. The place soon had a few shooting scrapes, and the excellent marksmanship of the day contributed to the start of the traditional boothill graveyard.

Trail City got off to such an optimistic start that it inspired a rival—just barely inside Kansas and twenty-eight miles down south toward Texas from Trail. This was Borders, named for Joe H. Borders of Coolidge, Kansas, a banker and publisher and one of the promoters of the town. Borders was on the cattle trail and a stage line. Its promoters promised a railroad and irrigation canals that would carry water from the Arkansas and make a paradise of the dry Kansas country-side. This town started off with a lively little newspaper, *The Borders Rover,* and its first issue bubbled with enthusiasm. It reported:

Borders, Stanton County, Kansas, is the liveliest and most successful town in southwest Kansas. Situated on the state line, and is absolutely without rival or peer!

The Town Company, which is composed of the best element of the world-renowned town builders of southwest Kansas, have spared no means to make booming Borders one of the best towns in Kansas, and have built a hotel at a cost of $3,500, which challenges everything in that line south of the Arkansas River for comfort, beauty and architecture. The town is only a few months old, and can boast of two hotels, a newspaper, several stores, a large livery barn, blacksmith and tin shop, and several very good residence buildings. Shade trees consisting of catalpa, walnut and boxelder have been ordered and will be planted on all the streets of the town.

But not many editions later (in August of 1887), *The Borders Rover* changed its happy tune, and its editors were ready to rove around looking for jobs elsewhere. The paper reported: "The Trail . . . adjoining Stanton County on the west, is being rapidly taken up by settlers."

At about this time, *The Citizen* at Coolidge had a significant report: "While more than 90,000 [Texas cattle] were sold at Trail City during the season [1887], at least 70,000 were returned to their home state."

The Range Journal of Denver reported conditions a bit more picturesquely: "The cattle that have come north this year have not found a market, and several herds have turned their tails to the home of the aurora borealis, and are marching back to the Panhandle of Texas."

An act that had taken place in faraway Washington on August 4, 1886, was sealing the doom of the cow business as men in Texas and the Southwest had known it. On that date, the Congress had authorized establishment of the Bent Land District. This was a chunk of country in Colorado seventy miles wide and one hundred forty-five miles long. A federal land office, to serve homesteaders, was opened in Lamar, Colorado, on the first day of 1887. The vast stretch of country, across which the skull-marked National Cattle Trail ran, was opened to settlement on July 25, 1887, just after the season's run of cattle had passed.

The Sentinel of Garden City, Kansas, reported: ". . . It is the choice land, and there was a perfect stampede for it. . . ."

The controversial National Cattle Trail was never successful, and every drive over it was a battle; it came too late in the game, as did Trail City and Borders. A few drovers, among them the die-hards who fought bitterly against change or closed their eyes to the hard facts of barbed wire, settlement and other cowmen, kept struggling to trail northward, but only for a short while. The big XIT stayed with the wide, grassy road longer than any other outfit. It raised steers on its Texas ranch and for a time trailed them to Montana, between the Yellowstone and the Missouri, for finishing. The XIT fought through with herds for a few years and then it admitted that the day of trailing cattle long distances had passed.

In the twenty some years of the open trail, ten million Texas cattle—forty million cloven hoofs—plodded northward and westward to market. Thirty-two thousand men, most of them cowpunchers who really knew how to throw a day's work, rode up the trails with the herds; in their collective *remudas* of zebra duns, grays, strawberry roans, blacks, bays and sorrels were untold thousands of horses. Rattling chuck wagons loaded with grub rutted the grass from the Rio Grande to Canada, and there were ashes of old campfires every mile of the way. Along the trails were lonely, unmarked graves, such as that of Burt Phelps in the Red River Valley.

Now the rattle of boxcars replaced the clatter of hoofs.

· 10 ·

Ill Winds

On the last day of 1885, Texas Red Cochran, one of the legion of cow-pokes whose home addresses were in their nicknames, was out on the range at the foot of the Black Hills in South Dakota—up to the north of what is now the Pine Ridge Reservation, the home of the Sioux. Being an ambitious leather-pounder, he had bought himself a herd of steers—two thousand three hundred—in his home state and trailed north to let his beeves graze and thicken their tallow. He had a lot of company from home up there. Northwest Texas cowmen and, in fact, ranchers from all over Texas had herds grazing everywhere in the grasslands West.

They had expanded to new pastures during the boom, leasing little and big worlds; the forced run from the Cheyenne-Arapahoe Reservation had further scattered the Texans, and now the drought had sent many a man herding northward in search of grass and water.

Thus spread out, the Texans couldn't be missed by any thing good or bad that hit the beef business—no matter where it hit. What happened to Texas Red and his little herd in Dakota, to Slaughter with his vast outfit in Montana, on Dillingham Prairie or in western Texas, or to the Waggoners and Burnetts in the land of the Comanche would naturally affect every rancher in the West. This put Red Cochran in pretty pert company.

Luck had been with the enterprising puncher in his attempt to become a cowman. The grass was lush. The autumn had been mellow, and the early winter crisp and bracing but mild. At night in his lonely camp on the far range, Texas Red had looked up at the cold, twinkling stars in the sky; he had watched the weird glow and flashing of the northern lights. He heard the big wolves howl in the distance.

Texas Red, he related long years later, pondered many a night on the circumstances and the inner urges that made it seem right for a man to live in wild country a thousand or two miles from home with a bunch of steers.

He dreamed of a home range on the mesquite prairie at Belle Plain in Callahan County not far from where Mexia Creek wound among the rocky hills. He might, he calculated, get hold of a few thousand acres there and also keep a finishing range in the Dakotas or maybe in Montana. He dreamed—and in his reminiscence fifty-five years later the dreams were not entirely forgotten—of a stone house with white gables at the edge of Belle Plain—a ranch place like Tom Windham had.

A man could never get ahead more than a forty-dollar saddle and a red-eyed Saturday night in town by riding for the other fellow. But if he branched out, took the risk and became a cowman with his own herds . . .

The last day of the year was a weather-breeder. It was close, tense, oppressive—the sort that makes men and cows restless. There was a yellowish haze lying along the Canadian line.

By midmorning, dark clouds boiled up and scudded southward across the sky. A thick, soupy mist came down. Within a few minutes it turned to hard, sharp snow. Then the wind came shrieking out of the north. The temperature dropped below zero so rapidly that thermometers couldn't keep pace with it.

The Great White Ruin roared southward.

Texas Red was with his steers on the range. The minute the icy wind whistled around their horns, the steers bunched, turned tail to the storm and marched southward. In their path were deep gulches and high, sheer bluffs.

Yelling at the top of his voice and occasionally firing his pistol, Red dashed his horse to the head of the herd. His idea was to veer the leaders and gradually force the steers to move in a large circle.

The steers didn't veer. They marched straight ahead, as if they were blind.

By this time the snow was so heavy and blowing with such force that it seemed like a fog. Red couldn't see his horse's head. He kept at the steers by ear, fighting desperately to turn them.

He heard the leaders thudding down a bluff that he knew to be forty feet high, with piles of sharp stones at the bottom. The Texas cowboy who had put all his savings and his credit into one herd in an effort to get into business pulled his horse away from the marching beasts, and between screams of the wind he heard all his steers go crashing over the bluff. Because of the fogging snow he couldn't see the bottom, but he knew that down there was a mass of dead, dying and struggling steers.

The blizzard howled on south, leaving a path of death and destruction. In Kansas, two dozen persons in one county froze to death that night. The wind was so savage that it sundered prairie shacks. The people still living in dugouts were the safest.

At Fort Camp Supply in the Cherokee Outlet, six half-frozen horses pulling a stage staggered up to the station. The passengers, three men and a woman, were almost frozen, though they had huddled under heavy robes. The driver out on the exposed front seat was dead—frozen stiff.

Farther to the south in the Texas Panhandle, Les Cator ventured out on his ranch to see whether he could save any cattle. He came upon a settler's wagon. The team of bony sorrel horses lay dead, still in the harness and with the lines extending back through the small puckered hole in the tarp into the wagon. He looked inside the wagon, and his heart sank. Huddled together were the frozen bodies of a father, mother, and three small children.

At nine o'clock of the night the storm hit Texas, John Peterson was driving a two-horse stage to old Fort Elliott in the Panhandle. He had no passengers. Snow drifted into banks and the wind picked up billows of sand, making this a black blizzard. He wandered off the road and drove directly into an old well some five feet in diameter. Peterson made his way back to a station on Commission Creek near the present town of Canadian, Texas. A transient had found refuge in the station, and he was discussing the weather with Oliver Nelson. When Peterson told of his mishap, Nelson and the visitor figured it would be bad to leave a team dangling by their harness in the mouth of the well. They went with Peterson to rescue the team—a big horse known as Punkin and a lean, wiry mule named Kit.

Peterson had centered the well. The tongue of his stage had rammed into the opposite side. The men got ropes on the animals' feet, cut the harness and managed to yank them out of the hole. They skidded Punkin out just at daylight. They were almost frozen when they got back to the station and the comfort of black coffee.

Like Texas Red Cochran's steers, all the range cattle in the sweep of the blizzard tucked their tails, humped up, lowered their heads and drifted with the snow and wind. Any number of leather-lunged, six-gun-banging cow-pokes couldn't turn a herd when the crazed animals struck their blizzard gait. This time, hundreds of thousands of range cattle struck that gait, a relentless stampede extending for hundreds of miles.

A range cow isn't afraid of a man on the ground; neither is she afraid of a horse. But a man on a horse is something else in the cow's mind. The cow doesn't seem to understand that a man on horseback is a combination of animals. Apparently the cow regards the two as one animal—and one too powerful for her. So a single cow, or a herd, yields to a man on a horse—he is the master. But in a blizzard the cattle lose this sense of fear, and a man on a horse is almost as helpless as a man on foot.

On many a stretch of range down across Texas to the Rio Grande, the cowboys, braving the killing cold and the sharp, relentless horns and hoofs of maddened cattle, rode desperately to turn the herds and circle them to more sheltered terrain. And, as the surviving punchers said afterward, many an old boy mounted the pale horse in that storm.

In this blizzard, the settlers fared little better than the cowboys who tried so desperately to stop the death march of cattle. The wide land from Dakota to Mexico was sparsely settled—small towns, ranch headquarters, line camps, shacks and dugouts—and very few farming families had adequate protection against such a severe and sustained storm. No one could ever gather accurate figures on the deaths, but the estimates ran as high as three hundred.

The loss of cattle was never known; it was simply estimated in big percentages. Cattle crashed off bluffs, walked straight into bogs, piled up in ditches. In the early hours of the storm, before the lakes froze solidly, cattle walked out across the hard ice at the edges of lakes only to break through the thinner ice in the center and there pile up. Nearly every waterhole and lake was filled with cattle that drowned, froze or were trampled to death there. The shapes of these ghastly piles were round, rectangular, irregular—depending on the meandering of the shore lines. The Cimarron, Arkansas and Canadian Rivers were piled full of cattle. Ten thousand dead cattle were counted between Garden City, Kansas, and the White Woman River.

Cowboys reported that a man could walk from Kingsley, Kansas, to the Colorado line using cattle carcasses as a path and never touch the ground. Everywhere that there was an east-west fence, cattle stacked up against it and died, some of them still standing. Along some of these fences there were two to three layers of cattle extending back from the fence as far as one hundred yards.

Despite the numerous fences in southern Kansas, the Oklahoma Strip and the Cherokee Outlet, the most deadly trap in the West was the drift fence across the northern part of the Texas Panhandle. Back in 1882 and 1883, the Texans had grown tired of northern cattle drifting down on them during winter storms, and they had built this stout, four-wire fence to turn, or stop, them. Starting at the Indian Territory (Oklahoma) west line, the fence stretched westward one hundred and seventy-five miles to the eastern border of the Territory of New Mexico. Oliver Nelson, who cowboyed in Texas, Kansas and the Oklahoma Strip, said he saw cattle stacked up north of that fence after the big blizzard in piles four hundred yards wide. The cattle looked as if they had bedded down. In places where there were high drifts of snow only the horns of the dead cattle showed. Cattle from as far away as middle-Kansas hit the fence.

John Hollicot, manager of the LX Ranch in the Texas Panhandle, and his men skinned two hundred and fifty cattle to the mile for thirty-five miles along the fence. A merchant in one small town bought nearly forty-five thousand hides in the spring. Cowhides went to market by the trainload; there were no other marketable products on the prairies.

When the wind and snow ceased, the marching cattle that somehow had survived stopped and looked for feed, but there was none. The grass was covered with a heavy blanket of snow and ice. Horses pawed through the ice and found grass to nibble, but the cattle could only hump up and bawl. For days the waterholes were frozen over, and there was only snow to drink and eat. Many cattle starved. Lobo wolves, thirsting for warm blood, attacked the helpless animals.

While marching with their heads down, many of the cattle had collected great balls of icy snow on their muzzles. The balls had two gimlet-sized, dirty holes made by breathing. The feet of some of the survivors froze and broke off. Cowboys saw numerous cattle with legs frozen; when the weather warmed a bit those legs broke off at ankle or knee. Some of the cows tried to walk around on the stumps for a day or two before going down.

In the spring roundup, Red Cochran found fewer than fifty of his steers. He was broke; more than that, he was head over heels in debt. It was back to the saddle for him, pounding leather for the other man.

But there weren't too many "other men" left. In the early part of the year the Reynolds brothers had trailed seven thousand steers from Texas to their Dakota range, and they lost every steer. The spring roundup was a ghostly thing. Nearly every time a puncher roped a cow, or an old cow bumped against something or fell to the ground, her horns slipped off. The cowboys surmised that the horns had frozen through and through during the terrifying winter. All across southern Kansas, the Oklahoma Strip, the Cherokee Outlet and the Texas Panhandle many of the calves were scarred by wolf bites. On some of them, strips of skin two to four inches wide and a foot long dangled wrong side out; this skin had been peeled off by attacking lobos. One of the big jobs of the roundup was that of trimming off the strips of hide.

Seeing the ruin day by day, some of the boys became disheartened. One outfit stopped in Colorado City, Texas, to take on supplies. The cowboys were turned loose in town but ordered to be back at the wagon at a fixed time. One man didn't show up, and the boss rode into town to find him.

He located the cowboy in a saloon.

"Time to git to the wagon," the boss ordered.

"Who asked you to pray?" the puncher snarled. "I'm not going to the wagon."

The boss floored him with a right to the jaw. The waddy jumped and lunged at the boss, who dodged and let go a haymaker that really jarred the cowboy.

Looking up from the floor with his arms shielding his face, the cowboy said, "Boss, which away *is* the wagon?"

There weren't many calves in the spring. On the big D Cross Spread of J. M. Day near Ashland, Kansas, the boys branded nine hundred calves; the previous spring they had branded ten thousand from the same herd.

Not counting the extreme shortage of calves, losses in this blizzard ran from forty to eighty per cent, with many small operators like Red Cochran suffering an almost total wipe-out.

But there were other woes almost as ruinous as the frightful storm.

In the area of the Northwest Texas Association the force of the blizzard hadn't been as severe as farther northward, but nature added a slower but surer method of decimating herds and forcing cowmen to dig for their bottom dollar. By summer nearly all of Texas was beginning to burn to a crisp. Grass was scarce and water was scarcer.

The drought that had started the summer before continued its telling work and extended into the Midwestern Corn Belt states, where farmers and stockmen were short of feed, and then widened into Wyoming and Montana. With hand-shaded eyes cowmen scanned the brassy sky for clouds. When, at last, the clouds came it was again winter and they brought only more destruction.

Cold weather arrived early. Blue northers whistled across the expanse hit by the big blizzard, and in Montana, Wyoming, Colorado and parts of New Mexico snow tumbled down time and again and thickened on the ground, covering grass and choking streams and waterholes. The cattle in that big region, which had felt the backlash of the storm of the past winter, had little to eat and they weakened. In December, one blizzard followed the other. None was so bad as the

Great White Ruin of the year before, but the constant cold kept snow on the ground and the icy north wind drifted the cattle. They milled along the shores of streams and gnawed the bark off trees, the only feed for numberless empty cow stomachs. Some of the cowmen managed to get tads of hay to their range by going out on sleds, but the attempts to feed were all but hopeless.

Charles M. Russell, one of the artists who had been attracted to the West during the wonderful boom period, was holed up on the OH Ranch, belonging to Jesse Phelps and his partners, that winter. One night Phelps grumbled that he had to write a letter to Louis Kaufman of Helena, Montana, one of the partners, who had asked for information on range conditions. While Phelps penned the letter, Russell painted a postcard-size water color picturing a ribby old cow humped up knee-deep in snow. A white landscape spread out from her. Circling her in the snow was a pack of wolves, licking their chops.

Russell suggested that Phelps send the sketch along with the letter. When Phelps saw the sketch he decided it told the story much better than his note and he sent only the water color—and in doing so started Charles M. Russell on his way to fame.

Russell entitled his sketch *Waiting for a Chinook*.

The chinook, the warm winter wind that often sweeps that country like a breath of sunny spring, seemed to be about the only thing that could save the cattle.

The West is full of engaging stories of that quickly executed sketch. Probably the most likely one is that when Kaufman saw it he went out and got drunk. Anyhow, he gave the picture to a saddle maker named Ben Roberts. If Kaufman had kept the sketch he soon could have sold it for enough to have replaced many of the cows he had lost. Up to that time he and his associates had seen some five thousand of his cattle die on the snowy range, and knowledge of this loss was pretty general around Helena and over Montana. For this reason, someone changed the name of the Russell sketch to *The Last of Five Thousand.*

But just the same, cowmen talked of, and prayed for, a chinook, the one great blessing that could come unheralded and bring hope to the highland prairies.

The chinook came on a day early in January of 1887. The day was bright, the sky blue, the wind wonderfully warm. It took the chill out of the air. It bathed the packed snow with melting warmth.

The tight kinks in the backs of the cattle began to loosen, and the half-starved critters walked through the slush in search of patches of grass. Then the chinook was wafted away, replaced by a mass of air from the North Pole. A hard freeze turned the slush into diamond-blue ice that sheathed the ground the rest of the winter. More blizzards thickened the ice.

Spring came late, but it didn't matter. On the highland range from the top of Montana (and deep into Canada) to the southern line of Colorado there was only gloom. The roundup that spring was the saddest ever. For the first, and only, time great flocks of turkey buzzards sailed in the Wyoming sky, circling slowly down.

Thomas Sturgis saw the big, craven birds wheeling low when, on a day in June, he sadly caught a Union Pacific train in Cheyenne for New York. He had hurried from the East to Wyoming in the lush days of the boom. He had become one of the big cowmen and had helped make a power of Wyoming Stock Growers and was secretary when the "chinook froze." Sturgis resigned that job. The Union

Cattle Company, a $3,000,000 outfit which he had headed, was gone. He went to New York to serve as chairman of the board of the American Trust, which was faltering.

Sturgis didn't stop by the Cheyenne Club. Bonds on that institution defaulted and sold for two dimes on the dollar; and the club, though it struggled along a few years, ceased to be a rangeland headquarters for the international cattle set.

The Swan Land and Cattle Company, which made the original importation of white-faces for the now world-famed Wyoming Hereford Ranch—run by Bob Lazear and one of his sons—went under. Nearly all the big outfits in Wyoming headed into quick liquidation and were no more. Up in Montana, Teddy Roosevelt abandoned his blizzard-swept, depression-struck spread and set out for Oyster Bay, San Juan Hill and the White House, his days of punching cows gone forever.

The shoe company in St. Louis that had bought a herd from Glenn Halsell for $340,000 sold it out to a cowboy who had saved his year's wages.

With northwestern Texas plagued by burned and barren range and dry waterholes, C. C. Slaughter sold at giveaway prices ten thousand cattle to the XIT, which was stocking its three-million-acre range. Ikard and Harrold, who had gone hopefully into Greer County with cows almost too numerous to be tallied, sold to whoever would buy and retrenched on their smaller home ranges.

D. H. and J. W. Snyder, now members of the Cattle Raisers Association, saw a million dollars go under in snow and burn out in drought. They had been in the stock business in Texas since 1857. They had been major beef suppliers of the Confederacy. In the "bust" years of 1871 and 1873 they had trailed their herds to Wyoming, thereby helping develop the new range country to the north and west. By 1885, they were operating cattle outfits from the Gulf of Mexico to the Pacific Slope. Just before the wicked weather they were offered an even million dollars for their holdings. By the end of that winter they owed nearly that much and were selling out, retrenching and planning to get back in the saddle.

Ike Pryor, a future president of the Cattle Raisers Association, was doubly hit—by blizzard in Colorado and drought in Texas. About all he had left was a batch of newspaper clippings from the St. Louis Convention—clippings of stories that told how Pryor, the orphaned cottonpicker, had become a great drover and cattle king, with ranches in Texas and Colorado, who could sell out for nearly a million dollars.

In later years, John Clay, in writing of his adventures on the range and in the livestock business, summed up the thing that had happened: ". . . It was appalling and the cowmen could not realize their position . . . It was a catastrophe which the cowmen of today who did not go through it can never understand."

Contrary to Clay's assertion, at least one Texas cowman properly understood the position of the ranchers. There was no doubt in this old rangeman's mind about the source of the more serious troubles; likewise, he took for granted that the good Lord was well aware of the sort of containers in which nearly all provisions came to country stores and to ranch headquarters. The cowman was on his knees at a prayer meeting called to petition for rain, but he took a short cut. "Oh, God!" he prayed, and his voice rose with every need. "Soften the hearts of people in the East to send us barrels of flour, barrels of coffee, barrels of molasses, barrels of meal, barrels of pork, barrels of beans, barrels of sugar, barrels of vinegar, barrels of salt, barrels of pepper . . ."

At that point in the plea a neighbor jabbed the cowman in the ribs and whispered loudly, "That's a way to hell too much pepper!"

A barrel of pepper would probably have been a mighty lot for the frontier shakers, but it would have been the only surplus of the good things of life in the cow county that year.

A good many people in the East—especially after the colorful, front-paged convention in St. Louis—figured that all cowmen were rolling in free grass and wealth, that they were barons with retinues of peons to do their mean chores. On the other hand, Western people habitually blamed all economic woes on "Speculators, Wall Street and Chicago"—all folks too hardhearted to let a cowman get an honest price for his beeves.

In these sad days, the Texans still had cattle, but a herd of any size was a liability. The drought-stricken stock were thin, and only grass or feed could make beef of them. There was no profitable market anywhere for range cattle like these.

Needing some income in its early days, the XIT Ranch rounded up a herd of one thousand steers and trailed them one hundred and twenty miles to Higgins, on the Texas-Cherokee Strip line, to the Santa Fe Railway. Shipping to Chicago started. The first load arriving there didn't sell for enough money to pay the freight. The ranch management telegraphed the trail outfit in Higgins to quit shipping and to drive the remaining steers back to the water-short range.

The boom that had been so savory so long was over. "Good and over," as Jim Loving remarked at the 1887 meeting of northwest Texas cowmen.

Since the downward trend in cattle prices had begun at about the time of the St. Louis whoopla, many a cowman expressed the firm belief that the break came as a sort of retribution for the prairie pomp and show of wealth at that convention. Other ranchers argued that the big doings in St. Louis created an unfavorable public reaction which affected prices. For whatever they were worth, these were horseback calculations.

One tangible cause of the price break originated in the White House. When Cleveland chased the tens of thousands of beeves off the Cheyenne-Arapahoe Nation there was no range to which all the ejected stock could be herded; consequently droves of them had been rushed to market.

Just before Cleveland issued his order, grass-fat cattle were worth five dollars a hundredweight; three months later the same cattle would fetch only three dollars a hundredweight, and lower grades were selling at $1.80, the lowest since the debacle of 1873.

By this time, the drought had crept into some of the Midwestern farm states. Short of feed and fearful to the point of hysterics that prices would drop more, farmers, and even dairymen, rushed their cattle to market.

With the consumer demand thus met, there was no need in the scheme of food supply for the lean Western steers. Sudden and wholesale liquidation of the recently rich big outfits flooded what little market there was. Yet the drought country ranchmen had to reduce their herds or see them die, and they sold at giveaway prices.

As in the case of previous cattle busts, the great division had come to the cow country—the boys were separated from the men, and this time the men were having to hold on for dear life. But by now there had been developed a breed of men who, like those who had met at Graham ten years before, couldn't be weaned from the saddle and the big cow pastures. In the cowtown of Jacksboro, where Jim Loving was running the headquarters of the Stock Raisers Association, the wife of a merchant asked another woman whether her husband, a member of the Association, would stay in the ranching business.

"Why, certainly," the lady replied, "he'd stick to cows if he knew it meant he'd go to hades in a gocart."

What the cow-pokes, and even some of the cowmen and ugly-tempered bosses, didn't know was that in far-off places like Chicago, Omaha, St. Louis, Milwaukee, St. Paul, Kansas City, there had arisen forces as strong as the Great White Ruin or the Big Burn Drought. This was especially true in Chicago. The stockyard system of trade had grown up. Commission houses were having a big say in the distribution of beef that came from the wide range. There were packers, mainly four of them, handling the beef, and there were lengthening railroads that wanted to haul cattle to market.

The cowboys could see some of the other forces that had struck the West—the shacks, dugouts, small fields and fences of homesteaders. One day that spring a waddy working for Kit Carter saw a man plowing a rich piece of prairie.

"Look out there, Colonel Carter," he said. "Looks to me like that feller's turning up the wrong side of the ground."

For the Texas cowmen, the storms—cold, hot and economic—that had swept across the rangelands were not all to the bad. The multiple disaster made some of the old animosities look childlike. Colonel Goodnight laid down his Winchester and signed up with the Northwest Texas Association. Ike Pryor, the southern Texan, also joined.

It looked as if the steady, weathered old Texans weren't whipped at all, but were getting together to ride out trouble again.

· 11 ·

"Let's Get This Straight, Boys!"

In the first tumultuous decade after organization Texas cowmen had survived the coming of barbed wire, the end of free grass, the closing of the open range, the expansion of the beef business to all the West, defeat in the trail fight, blizzards, drought and the depression which still held on tenaciously.

Their boom was over; their industry lay prostrate. Yet few cowmen thought of quitting; they thought only of how to carry on.

There was indeed more resourcefulness than money rolling about the range in 1887 when nearly every rancher claimed he was living on "the interest on what I owe." It was the sort of resourcefulness that Jim Edwards pulled out of his pocket in lieu of dinero one broiling day when the plains of Texas were quivering with heat.

Edwards and his brother, Bill, had been running cattle in the arid Pecos country. There, while scouting around, Jim Edwards had found an old Indian burial ground and dug up a skeleton. He put the dried bones in an empty flour sack. With the sack under his arm—for he wanted to show his family and friends what he had found—he boarded a train for home a short time later.

In time the conductor came through the car collecting tickets. Not until then did Edwards realize that he hadn't bought a ticket and that he had failed to take along enough money for one.

"What do you mean getting on this train without a ticket or money?" the conductor demanded.

"I'll tell you, pardner," Edwards said. "Me and my brother came out here together and the drought struck us, and he died. Now I'm trying to take his bones back to our old home."

Edwards opened the sack and turned it mouth downward. A skull rolled out into the aisle, and the other bones rattled.

The conductor was so overcome that he not only let Edwards ride free but apologized for asking him about the ticket.

When the cowmen plunged into the business of counting up their woes at their spring session of 1887, A. P. Bush, a new member of the Association's executive committee, introduced a word which he thought described certain conditions. City friends had visited his Pitchfork Ranch in western Texas one day, and the big event for the guests had been a noon meal at the chuck wagon. Along with red beans, stewed apricots, quartered red onions, canned tomatoes and sourdough, the cook served a batch of dried beef which he had fried in tallow. It hadn't turned out well and looked, tasted and smelled like overaged cracklings.

Bush eased around and asked the cook what the devil was wrong with the beef.

The cook grinned, wiped his face on his sleeve and said, "The taller was ransom."

The cowmen agreed heartily that a good many things seemed "ransom." Prices for cattle were at rock bottom, for instance, but the cost of beef to housewives was about as high as it had been during the late boom.

"Every day," said Kit Carter, who was serving again as president, "someone says to me, 'You cowmen must be getting mighty rich, considering what I have to pay for steaks.' How people can think that, I don't know, with steers hardly bringing enough to pay for their shipping to market."

The time had come, the cowmen decided, to raise unshirted hell and get the saddle on the right horse. The big packers and the railroads were in cahoots, the cowmen publicly stated. "While we face the weather and take all the risks of production as well as the blame for high prices," they charged, "these gentlemen enjoy easy chairs in comfortable offices, and there they are lapping up the cream."

Pocketbooks all over the country had been hit by the price of a steak to go on the dinner table, whether oilcloth-covered or laid with linen; consequently, the row the cattlemen raised about the spread between the price paid for live cattle and the cost of beef at the butcher shop fell on attentive ears. Indeed, it created a national furor which raged for a generation. The old battle between St. Louis and Chicago bounced back into the news. Washington, which had been interested in the West mainly to the extent of keeping an eye on the public domain and seeing after the Indians, suddenly demanded to know what had happened to the cattle business. At the insistence of Senator Vest of Missouri, the United States Senate appointed a Select Committee to ride herd on range problems.

Senator Vest, who loved Chicago a good deal less than he did St. Louis, was named chairman. Serving with him were Senators Plumb of Kansas, Manderson of Nebraska, Coke of Texas and Cullom of Illinois. (Later Cullom was succeeded by Senator Farwell of Illinois, one of the owners of the XIT Ranch in Texas.)

For the first time since the St. Louis convention, the cow country hit the headlines; this was also the Association's first major participation in a controversy of national importance.

Old clear-eyed Kit Carter died about the time the verbal battle got under way—in 1888. Carter had never been the baron or cattle-king type. He was a man who wanted only to make a good and peaceful living on the range, and his quiet patience and wisdom had guided the cowmen and the industry through formative years. Many of the policies he established are a permanent part of the organization.

A. P. Bush, a graduate of the Universities of Mississippi and Virginia, took Carter's place as president. Ten years before, when the frontier cowmen had gathered under the oak at Graham, Bush was in the grocery business in Mobile and had never thought of owning cattle. But the boom out West had changed his mind, and now he headed the nation's biggest organization of range cowmen. Thus the younger generation was taking a front seat in the vehicle the old-timers had started rolling.

Compared with Carter and the men who had battled through the Indian wars and resisted the first great waves of rustling, Bush was a yearling. But he was capable of standing the gaff of boom and bust, and the cowmen admired him. They were not at all surprised when he wisely chose for his executive committee several ranchers who had had long and wide experience on the range. He picked Charles Goodnight, who knew by heart the ways of the West; Cape Willingham, who had been a noted sheriff in the roaring little cowtown of Tascosa, Texas; A. G. Boyce, an old-time drover who was then manager of the XIT; Murdo Mackenzie, the canny Scot who made the big Dundee-owned Matador a great empire;

D. G. Gardner, manager of Bush's Pitchfork Ranch; Sug Robinson, who had ranched all over the cow country; W. E. Halsell, one of the biggest cowmen in the Indian Territory; J. B. Wilson of Dallas; and Ike Pryor.

Some of these men, like Pryor, for example, were new members of the organization, but they knew all the straight and winding trails of the cow business; they were strong, determined men. Taking advantage of a wave of public feeling, they now hammered at the Select Senate Committee to get busy with its chores.

C. C. Slaughter had been champing at the bit to get before the senators, and when he did, he blamed the "beef trust" for the poverty that had come to Western ranges.

". . . I found that if I offered my cattle at Kansas City for sale," he said, "and did not sell them, as soon as I would go to Chicago, before the cattle arrived, it would be known what I was offered at Kansas City, and it naturally brought me to thinking that this is a strange coincidence. These fellows tell me just what I was offered in Kansas City, and they come up and just about offer me enough more to pay the freight, sometimes not so much. Then I would try St. Louis, and I found that about the same thing was going on there; that if I did not sell in St. Louis, and if I went on the passenger train to Chicago ahead of my cattle, the next morning I would find that the offer was known that was made for them in St. Louis."

J. C. Beatty of El Paso told a stranger story. He had started a little packing plant at El Paso and contracted to supply refrigerated beef to Los Angeles and San Diego.

"We continued the business until the railroad company refused to give us cars to ship beef. . . . We had to cease slaughtering, and the refrigerator plant had been shut down . . . except for the purpose of furnishing ice to the town.

. . . Along about the first of February Mr. Armour concluded that our business could not continue; that it was detrimental to his interests. This is the general understanding . . . The moment Mr. Armour put his refrigerator beef [in California], we were compelled to turn around and ship our steers to Kansas City and sell them at a loss; and the same beef, I suppose, was sent back in refrigerator cars a distance of eighteen hundred miles to Los Angeles and San Diego."

President Bush, who was now pushing the fight against the combine, admitted that men like himself had contributed to the cattle bust—the piling of golden capital into the business when it was booming. "I was one of those who was attracted to Texas by the singular advertising the industry had received," he said.

Senator Vest hit harder at the packers than did the cowmen. He said:

I dislike, in the discussion of a great question like this—for it is a great question—to say anything that has the least appearance of local interest, but I am compelled to allude to the fact that the largest city in my state, the City of St. Louis, which ought, geographically, to have been at least the equal of Chicago in the matter of purchasing and shipping cattle, is today far behind Chicago . . . But St. Louis has been stricken down. . . .

The city in which I live, Kansas City, is today in close alliance, so far as the cattle interest is concerned, with Chicago. But Chicago is the heart, blood, brain, liver, of the cattle trade throughout this country and throughout the world . . . We know that today five firms in the City of Chicago control the price of beef throughout the whole United States. There is not a butcher in the City of Washington who is not subservient to that combination in Chicago; not one from Boston to Charleston but who feels the effects of this combination. The great railroads running into Chicago are in the interest of this combination. . . .

Any bunch of cattle that goes from any portion of the West, and all go to Chicago, the moment they are shipped these gentlemen at Chicago are apprised of the quality, the number, when they will arrive, and are prepared with a price. . . . The shippers who bring cattle to that market must take those prices or let the cattle die, or ship them back.

Senator Cullom had about the same idea, saying, "This is not the result of a year or two's operation; it is the result of certain forces which have been going on for years. The control of the live stock business in the United States is centered in a few hands. . . ."

The star witness was for the defense—Phillip D. Armour. He blamed overproduction on the vast, big-company-financed ranges for the slump in prices.

". . . There has never been any combination or agreement of any kind between the firm of Armour and Company, of which I am a member, and any other party or parties, to fix the price which we should pay for live cattle, or to control the price which should be paid therefor," he said, "nor has there been any attempt on the part of this firm, in connection with others engaged in the dressed-beef business, or

with other purchasers of cattle, to control or depress the market for cattle. The firm of Armour and Company is not in any combination . . . with shippers of beef in the carcass, to fix the price for which beef carcasses shall be sold.

". . . I think there have been a great many people beyond cattlemen who, seeing this big decline, have believed there was something wrong and that the Big Four was a Jesse James."

This first fist-shaking at the packers and the railroads didn't repair the price of cattle, but it did herald the coming of the trust-busting days and a later battle. Nearly everybody had something bad to say about the combines.

Texas, under the governorship of Indian Fighter Sul Ross, brother-in-law of Kit Carter, passed its first antitrust laws. When the cowmen gathered for their 1888 meeting, they had a telegram from the Dallas headquarters of the Farmers Alliance and the Knights of Labor. Seeing an opportunity for public appeal, the two organizations proposed a co-opera-tive system of refrigerating and distributing beef—"object being to get a fair price for beef and reduce the price to the consumer."

Not wanting to bypass anything that might help their business, the distressed cowmen appointed C. C. Slaughter to confer with the Alliance and the Knights, which at that time had on a campaign for "homes for the homeless, land for the landless." Moreover, the cowmen lined up with public thinking with a pointed little assertion:

We are opposed to any and all combinations which attempt to control the price of food. We are also opposed to pools of rail-roads.

Once started on the business of raising hell with the mid-dlemen in their business, the ranchers jumped on everything that looked like abuse. The Union Stockyards at Chicago had a fixed dockage of five dollars on every beef animal with a broken rib.

"This broken rib steal," the cowmen accused, "is worse than highway robbery. The big packers hire their own dockers, and they are the sole judges of whether there is a broken rib. We demand that this be stopped!"

This strange method of fighting with words perhaps increased the tears sincerely shed for the days when cattle were trailed to market and sold immediately for gold, and the middleman had no place in the scheme of things. Certainly the perplexing experiences cattlemen underwent in submitting their cattle to train travel made the old adventuresome times seem dear in retrospect.

Henry H. Johnstone rode out one of these newfangled perplexities. He was a Britisher who had come out from Scotland and made good in the cowlands—and was never referred to as a "velvet britches." One fall he helped round up a bunch of cattle and take them to the railroad stop for shipment via cattle train. Later, to W. J. Todd, a friend living at Maple Hill, Kansas, Johnstone wrote a letter that was a tear-jerker for a cowman, though it had a gentle ending:

The herds of half a dozen owners were being held in the neighborhood of the stockyards of a small town on the Santa Fe Railroad. The cars were ready and the loading of the cattle was set for the following day. We had had some trouble from stampedes, but so far none of the herds had escaped.

I was on fourth guard when clouds began to gather and at the first blast of lightning and crash of thunder our herd bolted. My partner was riding at full speed some ten yards ahead of me and incessant flashes of lightning showed him spurring furiously in an effort to swing the runaways into a "mill." My own mount was on the dead run when he gave a desperate bound and I caught a glimpse of my companion and his horse rolling on the prairie as we cleared them. I had no time to make inquiry as to casualties as I had urgent business on hand. Ere long I was riding close to the lead cattle and pushing them off a straight course.

I was congratulating myself on having headed the stampede when a flash of lightning showed me another of the herds standing still and listening to the thunder of our approach. Another moment and our cattle ran into them. The shock of the collision was tremendous and a number of the other herd were knocked head over heels. The whole lot joined in the mad rush, presently running into another and yet another bunch until all the different herds were mingled and chaos was complete. The gray of dawn was now showing and the night herders along with reinforcements from the various camps were able to prevent the cattle from escaping altogether.

Before long my boss rode up and, after volubly cursing the cattle business and all things pertaining thereto, enquired, "Where's Stuttering Ike?"

I replied that his horse had fallen with him while trying to head the cattle. He then said, "You better go and back and pick up the pieces, then hit the high places for camp and get you a fresh horse."

I accordingly rode back over the ground I had recently covered at break-neck speed and soon made out a figure hobbling toward me on foot which proved to be my missing partner carrying his saddle and bridle.

I hailed him and asked him what had become of the horse, to which he replied, "The poor old plug has broken his dub-dub-damned neck," and burst into tears partly of sorrow and partly as a result of the shock of his tumble.

The light was getting stronger and I could see the smoke ascending from our campfire and the saddle horses rounded up. I galloped off toward camp while Ike followed, blubbering in a fashion quite in keeping with his usual method of articulation. On reaching camp I caught another horse and rode back to the cattle. The "captain" of the roundup, the various cattle owners and their foremen sat on their horses in a group by themselves and I rode toward them with the intention of reporting to my particular boss for instructions. When I came within earshot and heard some of the language being used I decided that the moment was not propitious in which to present myself.

It was now raining heavily and I rode over to one of our men who was sitting on his horse drenched to the skin with a stream of water running off the brim of his hat. To my inquiry as to what was the next move he replied curtly, "Damfino."

I meekly remarked that I did not understand the Cherokee language and if he could not speak English he had better make signs. At this point in our conversation I caught a glare in his eye which warned me that I was treading on dangerous ground so I removed myself to the far side of the seething thousands of cattle where I was well out of pistol range.

There were some 7,000 cattle in the maelstrom of animals and they still continued to run but heaving flanks and lolling tongues told that they were far spent.

In an hour or so we were able to cut off a couple of thousand which we proceeded to separate in accordance with brand and ear-mark.

The remainder of the cattle were allowed to scatter and graze with some of the men in charge of them. When the first lot were divided according to ownership, they were watered and grazed until nightfall when they were corralled in the stockyards, each lot in a separate enclosure. It took three days' of hard work to rectify the "mix-up" caused by the stampede and we were all devoutly thankful when the last trainload pulled out for the East . . .

When a herd of this kind eventually reaches the feed lots of the farming states they are quite likely to have an attack of nerves and to bolt across the fields, tearing down fences as they go, but before very long they settle down and devote their energies to the consumption of maize, kaffir and hay.

Then there was the Englishman who had followed the call of the West rather than the call of the sea as so many of his young fellow countrymen did. He wrote:

Stampedes by night do not occur very often and there is an undescribable charm in riding round and round a herd of cattle lying in peace under starlight skies, passing and repassing one's companion on night guard, sometimes exchanging a word or two but more often meeting and riding on in silence. A gentle breeze from the mountains cools the air and no sound is audible save the low breathing of the cattle or the distant wail of some wondering coyote. Such a scene doubtless inspired "The Cowboy's Prayer" written by a cowboy. The opening verse is as follows:

"Oh Lord, I've never lived where churches grow
   I love creation better as it stood
That day You finished it so long ago
   And looked upon Your work and called it good.
I know that others find You in the light
   That's sifted down through tinted window panes
But still I seem to feel You near tonight
   In this dim, quiet starlight on the plains."

Another puncher, Tex Bender, known as the "Cowboy Fiddler," wrote about the questionable joys of life while "railing" the cattle to market behind the lead steer of a coal-eating, smoke-belching engine. The boys had to get what accommodation they could in the caboose, which was often jam-packed with railway officials. And this new method of "getting there" didn't increase the amount of sleep the boys could grab, for at every halt the men had to jump out, one with a lantern and others with goads, walk along the rough ballast and peer into each car to discover beasts which required stirring up.

"Having found an offender," wrote Tex, "you poke her, prod her, twist her tail and do your utmost to make her rise. In the middle of your efforts the bell rings, the train starts; you clamber up the side of the car onto the roof, and when there make the best of your way back on the top of the train to the rear car. This little trip in the dark is not one to enjoy. There may be twenty cars, say forty feet long each. Before you have crossed two or three the train is going at full speed. Only one man has a lantern; you are incommoded by a heavy greatcoat, as the air at night is keen; the step from car to car requires no more than a slight spring; but it is dark, or, probably worse, the nerves are making your knees feel weak. It is a hard alternative; to get back to the caboose, or to sit down in the cold on top of the train until you reach a halting place; having tried both, it seems that neither can be cheerfully recommended. If you do not climb onto the roof you must take your chance of jumping onto the step of the last car as it goes by; this would be the reasonable way if you were allowed to do it; but as the engineer does not care to look back, you must consider whether you are sufficiently an acrobat to rejoin. Having reached Chicago there is an end of the business; the cattle are turned into the big stockyard, and sold by commission."

Another old cowboy called Dock didn't have to worry about lurking Indian war parties, but in a letter he posted from Caldwell, Kansas, written to the manager of the Swenson Ranch back in Texas, he reported on some complications his cattle train encountered:

Dear Sir: 6:30 this morning in going to the stockyards to feed at this place another train run into my stocktrain. On an open switch & killed 2 cows and crippled 4, & the rest of the cows in that car is now all over town, so I got one car less & a few cows in another car is feeling sore & some of them only got one horn left.

The crew of both train jumped off & myself, so it was no one hurt. It was not enough left of the engine & one stock car to tell the Fait. 8 or 10 of the Kansas cowboys is out all overTown picking up our Cattle—wish you could see them coming down the street driving one or two of them cows—I think they got 10 of the cows in a Pen (down in town) & they heard of 5 cows in a cornfield just a little while ago, so I guess they will get most of them back today. I will leave here about 5 P.M. will make to-morrow market.

Yours truly, Dock.

P.S.—This R.R. ought to take charge of this whole shipment & pay for same.

P.S.—The Sheriff shot one cow on the street just a little while ago.

P.S.—The cows down in town is making the horses run off with buggys and running all the women out of town.

P.S.—I think this will cost the R.R. a good deal in this town.

P.S.—The Rail Road they give me a poor & sorry run.

P.S.—They run my cattle 40 hour before this happened without feed.

While in a swatting mood the ranchers aimed a "P.S." blow at the commission houses, which had a charge per head for selling cattle on the major markets. Under this system, it cost a cowman as much to sell a sorry, light-weight steer as it did an animal graded prime beef, and the Association demanded (and successfully) that commission charges be on a percentage rather than the per-head basis.

The cowmen wound up their "let's get things straight, boys" session by virtually declaring a war of independence from Chicago and the markets that city seemed to control. They swore they would campaign for a union stockyards and a packing plant in Fort Worth.

They also had some words of advice for the President and the Congress of the United States, urging that it was the worst possible time even to consider opening up any part of Oklahoma to white settlement.

George Reynolds was strongly against measuring off that fine range in hundred-and-sixty-acre plots, but he had a hunch that the President and the Congress weren't going to pay much attention to the Cattle Association at that time. So Reynolds, who had branched into banking in his home town of Albany, lined up with the fifty thousand folks who made the sensational "home run" on the afternoon of April 22, 1889. He made it to Oklahoma City, where people were starting the town. Reynolds up-ended a couple of empty whiskey barrels, laid some rough boards across them and started banking. His enterprise developed into the First National Bank of Oklahoma City.

The fact that the United States government paid no attention to their Association's plea and went ahead and farmered the Oklahoma Territory didn't deter the cowmen. They came out strongly against "further settlement" of the Indian lands, mainly the Comanche-Kiowa country, the Cherokee Outlet and the Cheyenne-Arapahoe Lands.

This airing of views and lifting of voices was not earth-shaking, but it had a certain significance in that it represented something of a grass-roots revolt. Cattlemen were demanding fair play.

Except in a few instances, Westerners got along better among themselves, the old geographical differences that arose during prosperity subsiding in hard times.

Though the grass was scant and the price of cattle low, rustling increased in depression times; invariably that has been true since 1877. In such times, in addition to brand-burning and the work of professional thieves, men steal cattle to get a few subsistence dollars, or to get beef to put under empty belts.

A. P. Bush told of a stockman neighbor of his who rode up on a man who had just killed one of the rancher's yearlings. This made the stockman so angry that he started to shoot. But the other made no effort to fight or run; he just stood there.

Questioned by the wondering stockman, he said, "You caught me dead to rights, mister, and I'm ready to go to jail, but I wish you'd let me take some of this beef to my wife and baby back over there—at my wagon." The cowman went with him to the wagon—an unpainted old butcher-knife type covered with a dirty ducking sheet. Two bony horses nibbled at the almost barren ground and switched lazily at flies. In the wagon, lying on worn quilts, were a young woman and a little girl, both exhausted, apparently from starvation.

The rancher took the family home with him. The woman and child were nursed back to health, and the horses were given the first grain they had tasted within a year. When the settlers were ready to continue their journey "back home" the rancher gave them a few dollars.

There were hundreds like this family—people who had sold out and ventured by covered wagon to the promised land of plenty in the West, only to find it parched.

The hard times spurred the cowmen. With their rustler-chasing system and their strong, vociferous stand on Eastern "cream-lappers," they gained strength.

R. J. Kleberg, Sr., whose father carried a musket in the battle of San Jacinto, joined the Association, bringing to it the old and growing King Ranch. Men like R. B. Masterson and C. T. Herring also came into the organization. Masterson and Herring—both of whom built great cattle empires which still operate—were known as natural-born cowmen.

When Masterson was a lad in central Texas, his lips were extremely sensitive to wind and sun and often were raw and sore. The home remedy for such an ailment was a coat of copperas on the raw places, and this burned like brimstone. When Masterson's family would attempt to doctor his lips, he would break loose and run off.

One day his father offered to give him a calf if he would stand still for the copperas.

The boy stood still, while large, round tears ran down his face. From then on he never objected to copperas when there was a calf in it. Starting with the herd he acquired in this way, he became one of the biggest cowmen in Texas. Old-time ranchers still say that Masterson had the perfect formula for getting rich in the cattle business; it was: "Buy low and sell high."

C. T. Herring was orphaned when he was thirteen years old, but he never worked a day in his life for another man. He started farming in central Texas on a small scale. When he was sixteen he joined a party that planned to travel to California by way of Old Mexico. The party went broke and disbanded near Matamoras. Young Herring swapped personal effects for a horse and rode alone back to central Texas and more farming. From that he branched into the cattle business, and by 1893 he was running twenty thousand head on a hundred and seventy-five thousand acres which he leased from the Comanche-Kiowa Nation.

Later in the Texas Panhandle, where he owned the famed LS Ranch, Herring realized the curious dream of many a cowman—that of building a fine hotel; he put up the Hotel Herring in Amarillo.

Cowmen like Kleberg, Masterson, Herring, and all the rest in the growing band, never lost sight of their main objectives, and these things were pretty well rounded up in "The Cattleman's Prayer," which was published in live stock journals:

Now, O Lord, please lend thine ear, the prayer of a cattleman to hear. No doubt my prayer may seem quite strange, but I want you to bless our cattle range; bless the roundups year by year, and don't forget the growing steer.

As you, O Lord, my herd behold, it represents a sack of gold; I think at least ten cents a pound should be the price the year 'round. One thing more and then I'm through—instead of one calf, give my cows two. I may pray different from other men, but I have had my say, and now, Amen!

Texas Cattle Raisers

The cattlemen bristled with purpose when they met in the spring of 1893—the year of the great money panic, which started in Eastern financial districts and swept across the country like a shrieking blizzard. This was also the year that the threat to quarantine all Texas cattle because of the old bugaboo, Texas fever, grew more resolute. The Cherokee Strip in Oklahoma was opened to settlers and the amount of grazing land was again reduced. And certainly no prayers for "ten cents a pound" had been answered.

Nevertheless, there was a show of zip and zing among the ranchers. They had been in tight places many times before, and they were ready to find humor in their situation and laugh at themselves.

Ike Pryor told of a cowman friend in southern Texas who went to a lawyer to have his will looked over.

"How's this?" asked the lawyer. "You've named six bankers in this will to be your pallbearers. Of course, it's all right, but wouldn't you rather choose some friends with whom you are on better terms?"

"No, Judge, that's all right," the rancher said. "Those fellows have carried me so long they might as well finish the job."

C. R. Breedlove, who liked to spin yarns and express pointed opinions in conventions, regaled the stockmen with a story he thought was a better picture of the cowman's precarious position than Pryor's.

A cowboy had spent several nights in camp on the shore of the Llano. "One morning," he said, "I woke up and was having a little trouble breathing. Felt like a layer of bricks on my chest. I lowered my chin and rolled my eyes down, and there it was—a big, diamond-back rattlesnake coiled up on my chest with his big, ugly mouth not four inches from my chin. I was afraid that if I moved he'd peck me right in the kisser."

"Well, what did you do?" a friend inquired.

"Went back to sleep, and when I woke up he was gone!"

But the cowmen didn't sleep their threats off. The first thing they did was proudly change the name of their organization and extend it to take in a new world of cow country. The cattle business might not be blossoming like yucca on a wet May morning, but the Association was growing in membership and in influence. During the year a dozen small—county and district—organizations had dissolved and the members had joined up with the band of 1877. This was mainly because the Association had its detective force working expertly and because it had been speaking out effectively for the stock interest.

Seeing all the new members from all over Texas, from New Mexico and the Indian country, C. C. Slaughter got up and made a little speech:

We now operate from the banks of the Rio Grande to the boundary line of Kansas. Time was when we were a local organization. When we first met on Dillingham Prairie and determined to organize we could not see far enough into the future even to guess that on our seventeenth anniversary our little band would become the giant organization of today. We are the Cattle Raisers Association of Texas, and I move that we adopt that name here and now.

A great cheer went up, and there was no need to take a vote.

President Bush hammered for order. "A few years ago," he said, "our Association was on the decline, but it is now at the zenith of its prosperity, with a record of a million and a quarter cattle [belonging to members] on the books. And also on our records are the names of more than four hundred prominent stockmen. We are on our way."

The immense area covered by applications for membership that year showed how wide the scope of the organization had grown and how it had outlived its original title. The number of cattle run by prospective members had to be shown as the dues were five dollars a year and five cents per head on stock rendered. Applications were received from:

	Head of Cattle
J. W. Weaver, Indian Territory	600
Jules Washington, Indian Territory	2,000
Jones & Robinson, Indian Territory	400
A. J. West, Live Oak	700
Garrett & Collier, Hall County	
R. M. Bourland, Indian Territory	1,000
Live Oak Ranch Company	5,000
Hume Bros. of Austin	5,000
Jackson & Aldwell of Sherwood, Coke County	2,000
Barnett & Gibbs of Dallas	
W. T. Ward, Knox County	500
L. H. Pruett, Scurry County	500
John R. Lewis, Nolan County	1,000
M. T. & E. J. Johnson, New Mexico, Indian Territory	5,000
John Dennis, Eastland County	150
J. M. Campbell, Indian Territory	100
H. Windham, Callahan County	400
G. H. Ray of Texas	500

	Head of Cattle
T. J. Clegg, Eastland County	400
Jas. Funk, Tom Green County	2,500
Wm. Powell of Rhome, Wise County	
H. P. Reed of Lowell	300
Louis Runge, Menard County	2,000
W. W. Watts, Crosby County	3,000
J. V. Stokes, Midland and Ector Counties	1,000
H. C. Field, Menard County	500
C. R. Breedlove, Fisher County	100
Auson & Venner, Tom Green County and Osage Nation, Indian Territory	3,000
J. B. Polk, Hall County	500
L. C. Beverly of Clarendon	200
Rowe Bros. of Clarendon	10,000
T. A. Thompson, Runnels County	1,500
L. K. Purdham, Kiowa and Comanche Reservation	1,000
T. J. Hunt, Eastland County	500
W. A. Blackburn, Castro County	800
Cresswell Ranch & Cattle Company (Limited) Canadian	20,000
Jas. McLemont, Kinney County	7,000
J. G. Rice, Sterling County	1,000

Of course, each new member brought money into the coffers—money to pay detectives and inspectors, money to take care of the cost of trips to Austin, Washington, Denver or wherever the stock interest needed representation.

Yet it was not stock growers alone who now sought admittance to the Association. Aware of the strong organization the cattlemen had developed, other interests—among them, packers, commission people, financial houses, and railroads—attempted slyly to take over. In numbers they applied for membership, and they offered tantalizing bait—stuffed pocketbooks to provide lavish parties at conventions or to pay dues. But the cattlemen could not be bought.

Soft-spoken A. P. Bush praised heartily "the many friends of our Association." Then he made a suggestion that seemed routine and innocent—that there be no voting members except men and women who owned range herds. The cowmen made this an unqualified rule and put all other memberships on an honorary basis. They would run their own show.

Their next move was a major one. They voted to back with everything they had a government experiment on the King Ranch which was undertaking to determine the cause of Texas fever. This was one thing that had to be whipped if Texas were to remain in the running as a beef production state.

Also, Greenleaf Whittier Simpson of Boston was present at the meeting with a proposal to operate stockyards and a refrigeration plant at Fort Worth. In addition, he would organize a bank with resources of five million dollars—to make ranch loans at eight per cent interest. Some banks had been holding out for ten and twelve per cent on cattle paper. The only pledge the cowmen would have to make to enjoy the advantages of this new enterprise was that each member ship his stock to the Simpson yards or else pay fifty cents a head on all the slaughter cattle he sold elsewhere.

C. C. Slaughter was as fervent as he had been in organizing the cattlemen back in 1877. He couldn't stay off his feet. "I've been investigating this Yankee proposition," he said. "As a matter of fact, I've been investigating Yankees for some time, my second wife being one. I am raising a family of half-breeds.

"Let's join the Yankees. It means deep-water connections. We know New England people are thinkers and look out for their pennies. Let's invite them here."

So it was that Greenleaf Whittier Simpson of Boston received a rousing welcome for his project at Fort Worth—

the preliminary blows of a slugging match between the ranchers and Chicago and its packers and the railroads.

Ranging quite a way from the home pasture, the cowmen took a look at some national problems and edged into the international. They cocked their verbal guns and let go with a broadside at what they branded "the hair-in-the-butter mess"—the plan of big dairy interests to tax oleomargarine to death. They swore they would fight this plan to the bitter end, and they did fight it unceasingly for more than fifty years.

Then the rangemen came out without reservation for the proposed Nicaragua Canal. (They later backed their former-cowman friend, Teddy Roosevelt, in the successful Panama Canal project.)

Those forays out of the home corral ultimately led the stock growers into a showdown fight among themselves, the issue being whether they would ride headlong into controversial international matters that had political implications. This came to a tempestuous head some years later when the importation of cattle from Mexico caused an oversupply of beef and lowered the price.

At white heat over this competition, at least half of the Southwestern cowmen—and also those in the West and Middle West—were loud in their demands for a closing of the gate against Mexican cattle.

However, the executive committee of the Association warned against this, suggesting that semipolitical questions such as this one not be mentioned.

When this report was read, impetuous M. H. Sansom, the owner of one hundred cattle, who had joined the Association only the previous day, hopped up and shouted, "I move that we pass a strong resolution opposing this importation of Mexican cattle."

If lightning had struck the hall the old cowmen wouldn't have been more shocked.

Burk Burnett was the first of the founders to recover sufficiently to get to his feet.

"What *is* this?" he demanded. "Mr. Sansom joined us just yesterday, and, as I understand it, he owns only one hundred cows. Now he sounds off."

By the time Burnett sat down, Ed Fenlon of Midland was waving for attention. President Bush recognized him, and he said, "I have for years been a member of the executive committee. Only yesterday Mr. Sansom joined, and today we see him trying to run it. He has only one hundred cattle, while the members of the executive committee have 237,000."

And then Sansom took the floor again. "I readily admit that I joined yesterday and that I have only one hundred cattle," he shouted. "However, I have shipped more cattle than Burk Burnett. . . . With my one hundred cattle in the Association, I have as much right to talk as Burk Burnett with his thousands. . . ."

C. C. Slaughter, a strong believer in the rights of individuals, stood up and said, "Here is one member of the executive committee who believes that a new member with only two head of cattle has just as much right as any other member to express his sentiments."

This brought explosive applause, but Sansom's proposal was killed. By this time both sides had blood in their eyes and were itching for a showdown.

When the time came for electing officers, Burk Burnett arose and in as flowery a speech as a range cowboy ever made nominated Bush for re-election. Ike Pryor jumped up and, with a still longer speech, seconded.

Bill Hittson wasn't satisfied. He pointed out that Slaughter was the real daddy of the Association and that he had guided it through good years and bad, yet had been the chief officer only once—in 1885 when Kit Carter was sick. Hittson then nominated Slaughter for the presidency, and thereafter campaign speeches rent the air.

Finally a vote was called, and the count stood: Bush, 166; Slaughter, 129.

Then both sides made up, promising to ride together.

From the start, the Association had prided itself on being an organization that listened as long and intently to the little man as to the big operator. Through the years, the membership has consisted mainly of small ranchers. The convention argument involving Sansom, Burnett, Slaughter, Bush and others was actually an expression of the conviction of some of the younger men that the old policy of staying out of political controversy should be changed.

And in this the idea of the younger men and small operators prevailed. This little battle broke down certain barriers, and from then until now the Association has never stopped at state or international lines in making itself heard.

A few years later the cowmen stood and applauded when Slaughter offered this look at world affairs:

Whereas there are now in progress in different sections of the world, two great struggles in which the people of two well-established, free and progressive governments are seeking to assist and maintain their freedom and independence from intrusion, oppression and dictation or arrogant and cruel monarchies, therefore, be it resolved by the Texas Cattle Raisers Association that we hereby tender our sympathy and endorsement to the people of Cuba in their struggle for independence, and be it further resolved that we hereby extend to the people of Greece a hearty and cordial approbation of the action their king has taken to protect the lives of his subjects and dependents. . . .

A herd rounded up at the base of Sawtooth Mountain in the Big Bend Country.

An early dipping-vat scene. Many such structures were blown up in the Texas Fever War.

us men of the frontier, the range and the trail. From left to right, Captain John R.
es, one of the most famous of Texas Rangers in the borderlands; John Arnot, who
Scots lad emigrated to Texas to work on the Frying Pan (barbed-wire) Ranch and
big spreads; Ellison Carroll, the world's champion roper in 1890; Ab Blocker, noted
driver; and Bob Beverly, early cowboy in the Indian Nations, the Panhandle, New
co and the western Texas country around Midland—seen here as they got together
in the late 1930's at a convention of the Texas and Southwestern.

Will Rogers with John Carson and John R. Blocker. Here Blocker, who trailed more cattle to northern markets than any other man, is demonstrating the famed "Blocker Loop" for Rogers' benefit. (Photo by Smithers, copyrighted by N. H. Rose Collection.)

Range rig on the Matador. In this double buggy are John MacBain, who came over from Scotland to work on the Matador, and Harry Buchan, the Matador bookkeeper.

In town on Saturday.

The Scotland Yard of the range. Above, a present-day Texas and Southwestern field inspector camped near water—prepared for rough going or smooth. Lower left, the famed rustler catcher, John Russell, who served the Texas and Southwestern for nearly half a century as a field inspector and, eventually, chief inspector.

Chief of the rustler chasers—
Henry Bell, secretary and
manager incumbent of the
Texas and Southwestern.

Present-day home of the Texas and Southwestern at
410 East Weatherford Street, Fort Worth.

For nearly eighty years the cowmen have faced problems and fixed policy at their annual meetings. Here they register for their record-breaking convention, held in Dallas in 1951, when 2,671 cowmen crowded the meeting hall.

Ike Pryor made a note of this. When he returned home, he and J. H. P. Davis of Richmond, Texas, sent a special envoy to Cuba to keep them advised on cattle conditions. When the blockade was lifted at the end of the Spanish-American War, Pryor and Davis had a shipload of beeves on the way to Cuba. Buyers scurried around the Havana docks, bidding on the cattle, and they sold for prosperous prices. These were the first beeves to arrive in Cuba after the war. With their headstart, Pryor and Davis shipped in and sold seven thousand head before anyone else attempted to exploit this rich market.

In the rip-roaring session of 1893, the enterprising cattle producers intensified the war on rustlers.

One member said that the obstinacy of the thieves and their elusiveness reminded him of a herd of jackasses. This member passed around a copy of a bill of sale which had recently been tendered him by an old cowman in the Big Bend country:

Sold to R. H. Jones one lineal descendant of Christ's conveyance into Jerusalem for the sum of seventeen ($17.00) cash in hand. His age is unknown to the present generation, color twilight, guaranteed to be perfectly tame and docile, and easy to catch if handcuffed and chained to a mountain; otherwise it is easier to catch four aces.

The cowmen moved their headquarters office and Secretary Jim Loving from Jacksboro to Fort Worth. Moreover, they hired a full-time lawyer, Sam Cowan, to go into the scattered courthouses "from the bottom of Texas across to Illinois" and prosecute the thieves the range detectives and market inspectors caught.

They stationed their own private police all over Texas, in St. Louis, Chicago, Kansas City, in all parts of the Indian

Territory where range cattle still grazed, in Kansas, Colorado, New Mexico and Nebraska.

Discovering that some well-organized, smoothly operating gangs of rustlers were stealing cattle in Texas and the Neutral Strip and driving them into Kansas for shipment to feed lots, the ranchers stationed inspectors in the Corn Belt to see whether stolen cattle had made their way to these finishing grounds.

"My doctrine about thieves," volunteered C. R. Breedlove, "is push them 'til you get them in high water and then raise hell behind them."

Almost as if in defiance of the cowmen's new plan to fill the prisons with cow thieves, the rustlers struck all over the Southwest. A gang of men stole cattle by the herd in southern Texas and shipped them out by rail.

Inspectors hurried into the area. At one shipping point they saw a string of cattle cars on a siding, but no cattle. The inspectors hired horses and took to the brushy pastures

nearby. In a large thicket they found three hundred cattle being held for nighttime loading in the cars.

The inspectors seized the cattle and captured seven men who, during the year, were convicted and sent to prison. After one year with the new system—and the lawyer to prosecute—the executive committee reported: "So relentless have the prosecutions been conducted that this Association, in the vigor of its work, is compared with the United States government."

Not much later this statement wasn't considered too much of a superlative. Bush, the easygoing Southerner, kept getting reports of stealing and brand-burning in the Indian Territory. He lost his patience and ordered a full-scale clean-up.

Picked inspectors were sent to "invade" the territory around Chickasha. A dozen cowmen rode with these men, taking along horses, grub wagon and, of course, guns. In this fifteen-day campaign of riding the range and inspecting herds, the men cut out one hundred and seventy-five head of cattle, about half of them with burned brands, that had been stolen from Association members.

In the late years of the nineteenth century, the territory to the west—New Mexico—was a hangout for rustler gangs that made quick night raids on ranches in Texas and New Mexico and drove the stolen cattle into the hills. J. L. Dow, the Association inspector in Eddy County in eastern New Mexico, broke up half a dozen such gangs. On the strength of his record as a thief-catcher and a handler of bad men he was elected sheriff in November of 1896.

The next day his mail was full of letters warning him that he would never take office.

But on January 1, 1897, he did take the oath as sheriff. Immediately he went for the rustlers who had threatened him. On the evening of February 18, he walked along Fox Street in Eddy. A dozen guns roared; horses clattered away into the darkness. The new sheriff lay in the dust, cut to pieces by bullets.

At their next meeting the cowmen contributed nearly $2,000 to Dow's widow and children. They felt that Dow's good work with the Association had led to his death.

At about this time the Association detectives teamed up with the Texas Rangers—the state force of strong men that had guarded Texas, especially the frontier and the border, since 1836. At first there was some opposition to the Rangers because through the years of hard fighting they had won the reputation of men who shot first and asked questions later.

When, at one session, Ike Pryor and R. J. Kleberg offered a resolution praising and thanking the Rangers, L. F. Wilson of Wichita Falls leaped to his feet. "I'm against it," he said. "I have a cow thief placed on the plains. I told them [the Rangers] about it, but they have made no attempt to arrest him. I don't believe the Rangers ever arrested a cow thief. Two Rangers pulled their air-guns on me because I broke a quarantine, but they can't get thieves.

"By accident the Rangers killed a murderer in the Indian Territory, but they didn't know they had killed him," he continued. "They've shot a few bank robbers, but they can't arrest thieves."

Pryor pointed out that there were only four Ranger companies of eight men each; that they had saved cattlemen thousands and thousands of dollars by catching thieves.

Kleberg then joined in, "I think the statement of the man from Wichita Falls shows that we really need the Rangers."

The cowmen went ahead with their expression of thanks— with only one dissenting vote.

A. P. Bush served the organized cattlemen as their president longer than any other man; he built the Association into a unit of national influence, but he remained a sort of maverick and man of mystery. He was the only bachelor ever to hold the office of president, and this made him the subject of a good deal of gossip in the cattlelands of the Southwest. Nearly all of this gossip had a romantic angle—stories that Bush would return to the magnolia country one day and bring home to the West a Southern belle—the daughter of a banker . . . a rich widow . . . a society girl.

These stories gained fervor when Bush built a palatial, two-story white house on his ranch not far from the cowtown of Colorado City.

In 1899, Bush declined to stand for re-election. Not long afterward he sold his ranches and cattle and his banking interests and disappeared from the Western scene. Even his closest friends in the West had difficulty keeping track of him; about all they knew was that the long-rumored wedding never came off.

Bush spent his few remaining years on the Isle of Pines off Cuba, and there he died and was buried, far from the hot winds, the alkali dust, the gyp water and the clatter of hoofs of the cow country, where the ranchers were facing the challenge of a new century.

· 13 ·

Always a Pioneer

In the early days of the twentieth century the Southwestern cowmen were concerned with two kinds of Indians—those in Oklahoma and those in India. But the warpaths, like the Old Chisholm Trail, had grassed over or had been plowed up, and this time the troubles in Oklahoma were friendly.

Burk Burnett, Tom Waggoner, C. T. Herring and other Texans who had gone with their herds into the Comanche-Kiowa Nation had made their own peace with the Indians. The grass-leasing arrangement they had made—mainly through Chief Quanah Parker—was profitable for the ranchers and the Indians both, and, except for one titanic fact, everything was serene. That fact was that legions of white people other than the cowmen also wanted that land; they desired to be pioneer farmers out in the West.

Quanah Parker—son of a famed white captive of the Comanches, Cynthia Ann Parker—was on the side of the cowmen. As the last great Comanche chief, he, after years of bloody battles, had smoked the peace pipe in Washington and had become something of a celebrity in the national capital. For a time, there was only one Comanche-United States problem: Chief Parker had too many wives and Washington officials kept telling him that he had to reduce his household to the legal limit of one. On an occasion of such advice, Chief Parker asked how this could be done.

"Just decide on the one you want to keep," an officer in Indian Affairs suggested, "and then tell them."

The one-time war chief puzzled over this a moment and then replied, "You tell 'um."

In order to maintain relationships on a social as well as a business level, Burnett and Waggoner occasionally entertained Chief Parker and his friends at Fort Worth, putting them up in hotels and giving them parties.

On one of these trips from the reservation to the gas-lighted city, Chief Parker took Chief Yellow Bear, who stood high in the esteem of the tribe. When the chieftains retired to their hotel room late at night, Yellow Bear blew out the gas light.

When the chiefs failed to show up for breakfast, Burnett investigated. He found Yellow Bear dead and Quanah Parker barely breathing. Quanah recovered and returned to the tribe with the body of Yellow Bear. The Indians were suspicious, finding it hard to believe that such a thing as blowing out a flicker of fire would kill a man. They doubted Chief Parker's story, and he petitioned the cowmen for help. Thereupon, Burnett took some big bottles of smelling salts to Comancheland. He let leading Comanches sniff the bottle to see for themselves that the air which had killed Yellow Bear was really bad stuff. The sniffing Indians were convinced.

But this range-reservation diplomacy couldn't stand long against the swells of a westward-developing nation. All the Indian lands, except the rich Comanche-Kiowa country, had been settled, and in 1901 the gates were let down on that last big patch.

However, each of the some three thousand Indians was permitted to claim one hundred and sixty acres before the palefaces were turned loose; also, the Indians were to have a common range of four hundred and eighty thousand acres, this to be in two or three large sections. The common range was for the Indians' surplus cattle. The fact was that they had no surplus stock, and by some coincidence, nearly all the common range was marked off in one block, just across Red River from Texas. This was known as the "big pasture" and in it grazed the cattle of the Burnetts and other cowmen who leased it from the red men.

This was absolutely the last of the Oklahoma Indian frontier, but the cowmen, who had given up inch by inch, held on by their eyelashes.

Then Washington decreed that the fence around the big pasture must come down, and the cowmen were given a few months to clear out before the settlement runs started.

Burk Burnett and the Waggoners had been furiously buying Texas land, but Burnett didn't have enough acreage to take care of his cattle—if they all were moved to it at once.

Burnett boarded a train and a few days later turned up at the White House in Washington, accompanied by Texas' controversial senator, Joseph Weldon Bailey. The way Bailey related the event later, he introduced the white-hatted cowman to the President, Theodore Roosevelt.

"Glad to know you," the President said. "I've been a cattleman myself."

Then the big-pasture man explained to the former Dakota rancher how a quick move of his herds would be ruinous. Roosevelt listened attentively and agreed. He extended the deadline, giving the Texans an extra year to get across Red River before the white settlers took over the big pasture.

Having in the White House a man who had experienced blizzards and other problems of ranchers was helpful indeed. Down in the coastal country of Texas, Al McFadden was trying out a project that involved cowmen with the India

Indians. Starting with a Brahman bull, McFadden was breeding a new sort of cattle.

He added to his stock one day in St. Louis. While attending a circus at the World's Fair of 1904, he saw a Brahman cow and bull in a cage which was marked "the sacred cow of India." McFadden bought the animals for $1,000 and shipped them to his ranch near Victoria, and the Brahmans were established in Texas. Thomas O'Connor, a neighbor of McFadden, and Abel Borden, who was running the outfit of the late Shanghai Pierce, bought a few of the humpbacks from McFadden and still wanted more. They raised the money for a buying excursion into the homeland of the sacred cow. Borden and Dr. Bill Thompson of San Antonio made the trip.

Nearly every fine Brahman they laid their eyes on and sought to buy turned out to be sacred and not for sale at any price. They finally got together a herd of fifty cows and bulls and loaded them at Bombay on a ship bound for New York.

There Borden ran into trouble. Inspectors for the United States Treasury Department decided the cattle were diseased, and they were held in quarantine. Borden and O'Connor ranted and threatened the inspectors. They besieged their senators and congressmen, but the cattle remained in quarantine. By this time, six months after arrival in New York, only thirty-three of the Brahmans were alive.

Knowing of President Roosevelt's considerate attitude toward cowmen, Borden called at the White House and explained his personal problem of the sacred cows. A Presidential telephone call to the Treasury Department released the cattle within the hour, and the thirty-three Brahmans were soon grazing in southern Texas, sixteen of them on O'Connor's ranch and seventeen in the Shanghai Pierce pastures. This experiment started by Al McFadden was to bring a major change in the beef cattle business—and also to add a lot of belled rough stuff to the mayhem sport of rodeo.

On all sides, the new was gaining in the West and the old was passing—new breeds, new methods, new policies, new men.

On November 24, 1902, Jim Loving died—without ever realizing his dream of a rustlerless range. Of all the cowmen of the nation, Loving battled more thieves than anyone else. From the time he helped organize the Association on that chilly February day of 1877 until his death he knew only short periods of tranquillity in what was generally considered a peaceful pastoral pursuit.

At the fortieth annual meeting of the Association, J. H. Graham, then one of the few survivors of the original organizers, said:

"George Washington has been called the father of our country, and so should James C. Loving be called the father of the Cattle Raisers Association. . . . He ran the organization for years and years—as long as he lived. We all did just about what he wanted done and the Association grew."

At the time of Loving's death the newspapers and live stock journals, in reviewing the lusty quarter-century just passed, said that an era of pioneering had ended.

But if the cowmen's organization was losing some of its old strong men, it was gaining men who were just as steadfast, strong and determined. It looked as if there would always be a pioneer.

In the year of Loving's death, W. L. Kingston and his wife joined the Association, and he soon became a member of the executive committee. Up to that time, the Kingstons had never bought a pound of bacon or ham, a bucket of packinghouse lard or a cake of washing soap; they had produced all these necessities themselves—along with beef, potatoes, beans and even honey.

Like earlier cowmen, Kingston had longed for space and opportunity to do something on his own. He and his bride had set out for Arizona in search of ranchlands, but before they got out of Texas, Kingston saw some men slaughter a yearling that dressed four hundred pounds. He asked where such a fine calf was raised, and one of the men said, "Jim Duncan raised him over in the Davis Mountains."

"That's good enough country for me," said Kingston. And the couple turned their wagon toward the Big Bend country.

The couple had one hundred and seven cattle, their wagon and team, and $4.70 in cash. Kingston made a deal to buy one hundred and sixty acres and he leased about two thousand five hundred acres more. In addition to running his little ranch, Kingston freighted lumber to make money to buy more land. While doing this, he kept his eyes open to see just where cattle seemed to thrive best, and there he bought his land—some forty thousand acres of it.

In the lonely vastness of the Big Bend the scenery was of majestic grandeur, but there were perils in a country where

even in summer the temperature could change with alarming suddenness; and when all the trails were winding mountain passages, and the comforts and resources of town were accordingly even farther away than the considerable number of miles the crow flies. Yet cattle thrived in the high, dry air. The people who settled and loved the country—Pruetts, Britts, Mitchells, Jones, Kokernots, Jacksons and eventually the Reynolds brothers—developed "strength for the day" equal to the demands it made upon them, and the comradely spirit of neighborly aid had a stronghold there.

Mrs. Kingston was a turn-of-the-century pioneer woman who replaced those of the old school, yet retained their endless fortitude. "Mr. Kingston was away from home a great deal of the time," she said, "but I always found plenty of work to do and didn't just sit around and worry because it was lonesome.

"I remember Mr. Kingston came back from one of his freighting trips without part of his bedding, and I said, 'Why, you have lost some of your bedding.'

" 'No, I didn't lose it,' he said. 'I found a man going up the trail who didn't have any bedding and I knew he would run into some bad cold weather; so I just gave him part of my bedding. I can get along all right.' "

One experience Mrs. Kingston had when her husband was away—working for the old Toyah Land and Cattle Company —remained forever vivid. "Our oldest son, Lee, was four years old, and our next son was just two months old. Lee had been a little puny for several days, but I did not think it was serious.

"About four o'clock one winter afternoon I noticed that he seemed to be getting worse and was having trouble breathing. There was nobody at the ranch headquarters except Mrs. Robert Hurst and myself. I saw it would not do to wait for any of the men to come in; so I hurriedly saddled one of the horses with a man's saddle, wrapped Lee in a blanket, put a pillow over the saddle horn and started to Fort Davis to the doctor, leaving the baby with Mrs. Hurst.

"I guess you can imagine my feelings as I traveled over that lonely mountain trail with that sick boy in my arms and darkness coming on. About dark I reached the ranch of Jim Powell, nine miles away. I told him where I was going and he hitched a team to his wagon and drove to Fort Davis with me—at what seemed like the slowest rate of speed I ever traveled.

"We reached the doctor about midnight. I said, 'Doctor, I am afraid my boy has diphtheria!'

"After a hurried examination, he replied, 'I wish to God it was diphtheria—it's worse than that, membrane croup in the worst form!'

"He worked over the boy until about daylight; then he told me Lee would pull through. Leaving Lee there to be brought on later by his father, I had to hurry on back to the ranch to the baby."

With new men like Kingston and the rear guard of old-timers, the Association kept at its expanding tasks. J. W. Colston, who had been assistant manager, took Loving's job of secretary and general manager for a short while, and then Capt. John T. Lytle, who had been one of the great trail drivers, took over that office.

Strong men followed Bush in the presidency—R. J. Kleberg of the King Ranch, Murdo Mackenzie of the Matador, W. W. Turney of the Big Bend County, and Ike Pryor.

It wasn't long before all hell broke loose in Texas and also on the shores of the Potomac.

· *14* ·

Texas Fever

On a midnight, a few minutes before the moon would rise over a cluster of hills in eastern Texas, T. J. Rodgers, an inspector for the Texas Live Stock Sanitary Commission, and three other men crouched in the brush on a ranch. As they waited, they heard footsteps approaching and low voices.

A match flared in the dark. Rodgers shouted, "Let's get 'em, boys!"

One of the "boys" pointed a flashlight toward a cattle dipping vat a few yards away and its beam fell on four men. The four ran, shooting wildly as they headed for the bushes. Rodgers and his aides opened up with their pistols, and one of the fleeing men dropped to the ground wounded.

Rodgers raced to the dipping vat and jerked a sputtering fuse from a crude but potent bomb capable, if it had exploded, of blowing the vat part way to the moon.

Violence of this sort flared across Texas, set off by that old curse of Southwestern cattle—the Texas fever.

The United States Bureau of Animal Industry had laid down a quarantine on seventy-three per cent of Texas—all of it lying east of a line starting at the southwestern corner of Oklahoma and zigzagging far southward to the Rio Grande. East of that line, where the old Northwestern Texas Stock Growers' districts had been, and where some of the major ranches in the state (including Bob Kleberg's King Ranch) now lay, rigid restrictions made it next to impossible to market beef cattle profitably.

Eventually fourteen other states found themselves in the same situation as Texas and for the same reason. All of Louisiana was under hard quarantine. The hex of Texas cattle had spread to the four winds.

Experiments on the King Ranch—those the Texas Cattle Raisers Association had endorsed—proved that ticks caused the Texas fever; moreover, these same tests showed that systematic dipping of cattle in a solution strong with creosote could eradicate the pests—in a pasture, a county or a whole state.

So the mystery which in other hectic years Missouri farmers and Kansas Jayhawkers had thought was a Spanish curse or "poisonous halitosis" was solved. Animals in tick country were immune to the infection, but wherever they went they dropped the tiny ticks; these then crawled up the legs of other cattle, and practically always fever and death developed in animals exposed to the parasite for the first time.

Two trails, both rugged, were open to the cowmen—get rid of the ticks or get out of the beef cattle business. They decided without hesitance to eradicate the ticks, an undertaking they realized would be fully as difficult as swatting all the buzzing houseflies in the Lone Star State.

Bob Kleberg, who put in that first dipping vat on the King Ranch, started the mammoth task of ridding his million-acre range of the parasites.

"Ask any cattle dealer from Colorado, Kansas, Oklahoma or the Northwest why Texas cattle are not desired in those states," Ike Pryor said. "If the tick is the only objection, and it is, why not do away with it? Drive the tick into the Gulf.

With the tick a matter of history your cattle would have the benefit of the markets of the world."

This task of exterminating the trillions of ticks in three-fourths of Texas was under the supervision of the United States Bureau of Animal Industry and the Texas Live Stock Sanitary Commission.

The Cattle Raisers Association was responsible for establishing the Sanitary Commission and Kleberg was chairman; its office space in Fort Worth was furnished by the Association, which also often paid its bills when state funds were too lean. The Association had persuaded the federal government to locate the Texas office of the Bureau of Animal Industy in Fort Worth; so the forces for tick eradication were centralized under the wing of the Association.

The dipping program began as a county by county procedure, and the first counties to volunteer and rid themselves of ticks included those in the districts laid out by the Northwestern Texas Stock Growers back in the general roundup days. Later laws required blocks of counties, or zones, to be cleaned up in a fixed period.

The quarantine was dynamite from the start. Cowmen and farmers in the "clean" territory guarded the quarantine line with armed diligence to make sure that no infested cattle crossed over. A great many settlers were moving to the western part of the state and to the Panhandle, where vast ranches like the XIT were beginning to break up into farms. These settlers with their household goods, chickens and cows, and perhaps a flea-bitten dog trotting in the shade of the wagon, knew little about the quarantine line, and they blithely crossed from ticky to tick-free country—only to meet with the coolest of welcomes. The King Ranch experiments showed that although the tick could be exterminated by dipping, a clean ranch or county could immediately be reinfested if a tick-ridden animal walked over the ground.

However, the crux of the problem involved the farmers —and a very small number of the stockmen themselves who were "doubting Thomases." The average farmer had only milk-pen calves to sell, and he usually sold to a nearby stockman or to a local slaughterhouse; he didn't have to worry about getting animals out of state to a market. The ticks didn't bother him, for his cattle were immune to the fever and their presence on an animal didn't in any way contaminate its flesh or milk. The eradication program meant that all his dairy cattle, horses and mules had to be dipped—and so did fine, expensive brood mares. Frightened stock could be injured, or killed, in the chutes or the vats. The farmers didn't like the risk they were required to take.

At first legions of farmers gave a big country "no" and refused to dip. The state passed laws providing for Sanitary Commission inspectors to go in and dip the stock of any farmer who refused to co-operate.

A wisp of a lady in eastern Texas had a herd of fine Jerseys which made her a living. When Sanitary Commission inspectors (not to be confused with Cattle Raisers Association inspectors) came to drive her cattle to a vat, she said, "No. You can't dip my cows."

One of the inspectors, a man with a well-groomed mustache that twirled into twin half-moons on each side of his nose, explained things to her and concluded with excessive emphasis that her cows were going to the vat right then.

"If you are going to take my cows," she finally said, "I go along."

She mounted a horse and rode behind her herd and the inspectors. When the sad procession reached the dipping vat, she stood close by and watched her sleek cows being prodded up the chute and forced to jump down into the deep end of the smelly dip-filled vat. The inspector held a long pole which he used to push down the heads of cows that failed to go all the way under the "wash."

When the last Jersey had climbed out, streaming creosote into the draining pen, the little lady lifted her ground-sweeping skirt and from somewhere pulled out an automatic pistol.

"Now," she said to the inspector, her voice ringing, "*You* go through!"

He thought she was joking, but he changed his mind when he saw that the glint in her eye was as hard and menacing as that of the pistol. He stepped into the vat and started walking through. When he was midway, the lady picked up the prod and ducked him and when he came up, his mustache shed two pungent streams of liquid onto his chin. The man was sick for several days. Finally in desperation he had to shave off his whiskers to get the smell from under his nose.

The reluctance of the great numbers of cattle handled in the dipping program to dive into the slimy solution resulted in at least one invention—the electric prod, a sort of swagger stick equipped with a battery which shocked a cow when it touched her. One of the first of these lively prods seen in western Texas was used by a Sanitary Commission Inspector on a dipping day at the R. Cordwent ranch in Callahan County. Cordwent, a native of London who had become a good-sized rancher, furnished the corrals, the vat and the dip for all his neighbors; he wanted the surrounding farms and small ranches free of infection so that there would be less danger of ticks getting back on his range.

On that dipping day at Cordwent's Cross Bar Ranch headquarters the hills and valleys were alive with cows. Small herds, nearly all of them driven by farmers on foot, hoofed slowly up and down the cedar-lined country lanes. The various bunches of animals awaited their turn for a trip through the vat.

Several farmers drove in their work mules and horses, stallions, mares and colts. One farmer had a bay mare named Patsy which would soon foal a mule colt. He asked the inspector to take a look at the mare and see that she had no ticks and then to "excuse" her from dipping.

"It won't hurt her," was the harried inspector's only reply.

When the mare came up the chute she balked at the sight of the vat. The inspector touched her tail with the electric prod. She squatted, squealed and leaped into the vat, making a mighty splash. The owner shook his fist.

Just after the noon lull, the inspector leaned his prod against the corral fence and stood on the rim of the vat, bending over to test the strength of the dip. Patsy's owner quickly grabbed the prod and rammed it to the seat of the inspector's pants. He lost his balance and tumbled into the vat.

The inspector was armed, but he had a good sense of humor and he laughed off the incident there in front of the farmers who outnumbered him approximately thirty to one.

Tossing inspectors in vats, engaging them in fist fights and even shooting at them became frequent occurrences; these men—whose job it was to determine whether a pasture or a county was clean and to supervise dipping—became understandably wary.

One day Frank Parker, a Sanitary Commission inspector at Baird, received a telegram telling him to be prepared to dip nine carloads of jackasses. It was signed by W. D. Ellis. Parker figured this was some sort of trick and he bided his time. But not for long; within a few hours a short trainload of braying burros rolled in on the Texas and Pacific Railroad and was shunted off on a siding.

Parker filled his vat and dipped the strongheaded, stubborn donks. He almost had to pick up each one and souse it in the wash and then drag it out. At about this time, Ellis came to Baird. He had bought the burros from the King Ranch, he told the inspector, and was sending them to Midland, where they would be fenced in a new thirteen-acre lake, there to live, walking and balking at will, and to pack the bottom of the lake with their cantakerous little hooves so that it would hold water. The burros had to be dipped before they could be moved out of ticky territory, Ellis explained. What Parker thought of the idea was not recorded.

In the early days of dipping, Tom Waggoner of the vast Three D spread in northwestern Texas made the best of what looked like a bad thing. He had some men drilling for badly needed water—but they struck some black, smelly stuff.

"I'll just be damned!" one of the men swore. "Stock dip!"

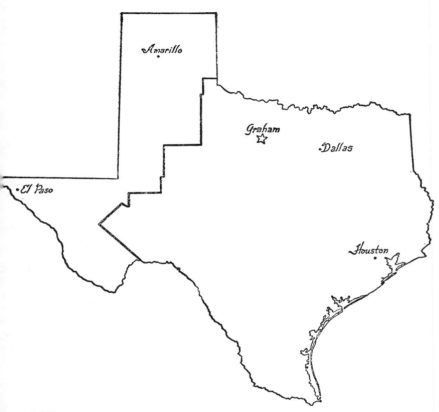

MAP OF TEXAS SHOWING FIRST TICK QUARANTINE LINE

The area to the right of this line was under quarantine and cattle could not be moved outside it. Only far western Texas and the Panhandle were tick free.

Waggoner was about as chagrined himself. He was reported to have remarked when he saw the high-grade petroleum, "Dad-blame it! My cows can't drink that stuff!"

However, Waggoner came out fairly well. He found that the oil, when mixed with more potent stuff, made an acceptable tick killer.

Perhaps the most nonplused man of these troublous times in Texas was Col. J. Sheb Williams of Paris. Having decided to invest in cattle, he traveled abroad to the Scottish Highlands and purchased seven fine Aberdeen Anguses for $1,000 each. When the shiny black cattle arrived in this country, Williams suddenly realized that his land was in ticky country and that if he put his cows there they were apt to die at $1,000 a whack. So he shipped them to a farm Senator Joe Bailey of Texas owned in Kentucky. Soon thereafter, Senator Bailey sold the farm, and Colonel Williams moved his cattle to far west Texas to stay until his part of the country could be freed of the parasites.

In the midst of the almost state-wide splatter of stock dip, W. C. Abbott of Brazoria County decided it was time to brag a little on the pests. At a meeting of cowmen when he was asked where he lived, he announced loudly and proudly, "I live in the coast country where the ticks get big enough to wear bells."

There was more violence, however, than fun. Farmers in almost every quarantined county ganged up in the manner of the wire-cutters of the early 1880's and went "vat-blasting." On one dark night thirteen dipping vats were dynamited in Cass County near Texarkana on the Texas-Arkansas line. This was sensational news, but the record didn't stand long. Shelby County in deep eastern Texas, where the ticks were really thick, had seventy dipping vats located at convenient points. A series of blasts—something on the order of a chain explosion—rocked the county one night, and sixty-nine of the vats were shattered with homemade bombs. The state sent two Texas Rangers to take over.

For a time the treasuries of the counties had to join the federal government and the state in contributing funds to the program; before this was changed, and financial responsibilities removed from the counties, local politicians ran for office and were elected on antitick eradication platforms. In some farming sections almost all the officials were elected as a result of favoring these platforms. In such counties as these it was difficult to convict a man or a gang for blowing up a few dipping vats. The juries would be hung every time.

The opponents of dipping resorted to thoughtful propaganda as well as violence. "How about the deer and the antelope?" they asked. "Are we going to dip them? Can't they carry ticks just like an old milk cow?"

Scientists of the United States Department of Agriculture got busy on that one and discovered a peculiar situation. Extensive tests were made on a California ranch where great numbers of deer played on the range. It was found that they did carry ticks in infested pastures, but when the parasites were eradicated from cattle the deer in the pasture were no longer infested. These scientists thereby proved that the cow was the only natural host.

This fight over Texas fever spread to the fourteen other states. After the quarantine was clamped on the whole of Louisiana, that state went into swift action; it built 3,478 vats, hired six hundred inspectors and killed out the ticks in one year. However, in Texas the work took more than thirty years—before finally the quarantine was lifted from the last of the state's 254 counties. Only a narrow strip along the Rio Grande is under quarantine today; before cattle can be moved out of there they must be dipped in accordance with Sanitary Commission regulations.

The severe violence didn't last throughout these Texas fever-fighting years. Some of the more disturbed farmers and stockmen became reconciled, and others, seeing that the program was good and profitable in the long run, joined in and helped put it over.

Ironically, the Texas tick proved a boon to mankind. Teddy Roosevelt couldn't have completed the Panama Canal without it. In a roundabout way, he was repaid for his kindness to Texas cowmen.

The Cattleman, the monthly magazine of the Texas and Southwestern Cattle Raisers Association, summed it up this way:

Texas fever has the distinction of being the first disease caused by a micro-organism proved to attack its victim exclusively through the agency of an intermediate host, or carrier of its causative germ or micro-parasite.

This somewhat restrained evaluation of the prowess of a Texas parasite big enough to wear a bell had some strong backing from other quarters. Dr. Salmon Flexner, who back in those years was with the Rockefeller Institute of Medical Research, said:

Our knowledge of the yellow fever would in all likelihood have been delayed if the work of the Bureau of Animal Industry of the United States Department of Agriculture on Texas fever had not been done. It has made possible such triumphs in sanitary science as has been accomplished on the isthmus of Panama.

Dr. E. C. Schroeder said in a lecture at Georgetown University in 1920:

The Panama Canal would not have been built if animal experimentation had not revealed the etiology of yellow fever. The

French failed to build it, not because they lacked intelligence, courage or perseverance, but because they did not know how to control yellow fever.

In the early days of the eradication process, however, the Cattle Raisers Association was definitely under fire; it was accused of saddling the farmers with a program of expense and destruction that was of value only to ranchers. Even some of the members of the Association pulled out in a huff. But the cowmen faced the censure without weakening in their determination to wipe out the old curse. Men like Kleberg, Pryor and Mackenzie had faced it—and also a good many other hard fights—for years and they were convinced that the majority would appreciate the results once the unpleasant job was done.

Out on the Matador, Murdo Mackenzie was in clean territory, and he figured that the only way to maintain that enviable but precarious condition was to exterminate the fever pest from the rest of Texas. Like A. P. Bush, he had entered the cattle business in the boom of the eighties. He had moved to the United States from Scotland in 1885 to work for the Prairie Land and Cattle Company, a Scottish syndicate in the Texas Panhandle. At that time, Mackenzie was thirty-five years old and knew little about cattle. Later he shifted to the Matador, another Scottish syndicate, as manager, and he became an internationally known cowman. He had an innate feel for the cattle business.

One of Mackenzie's close friends was Theodore Roosevelt. In his book, *A Book Lover's Holidays in the Open*, Roosevelt wrote:

During my term as President he [Mackenzie] was, on the whole, the most influential of the Western cattlegrowers. He was a leader of the far-seeing, enlightened element. He was a most powerful supporter of the government in the fight for the conservation of our national resources for the obligation without waste of our forests and pastures, for honest treatment of every-body and for the shaping of governmental policy in the interest of the small settler—the homemaker.

Mackenzie was as lavish, and more picturesque, in his praise of Roosevelt. He once pointed to a picture of a fine bull, Lomand Lad, hanging on his office wall and said, "Look at that head!" Swinging around in his chair, he pointed at a picture of Roosevelt on his desk and said, "Look at that head! Do you see the resemblance? Both heads have the same squareness and force of character. I want to buy and use on the Matador bulls with heads just like that."

This mutual admiration of a canny Scot on the Texas range and a New Yorker in the White House came in right handy. From the time the cattle trails were closed until 1903, when Murdo Mackenzie was winding up his time as president of the Cattle Association, the railroads had been calculatingly increasing their freight rates on cattle. The charges shot up alarmingly in 1903.

At this time the cowmen were in the midst of the Texas fever battle, but they knew the shipping rates on cattle would have to be lowered or getting their steers cleaned up and tick-free for the corn-belt feed lots would be in vain.

They filed a complaint with the Interstate Commerce Commission, therefore, asking that the railroads be restrained from hiking the rates—this, despite the fact that the federal government had never regulated a utility or fixed rates or prices. There was no law then providing for such authority.

Conscious of the fact that they were facing a hard battle, the Texas cattlemen went after recruits—to their ex-foes, the men who had fought them bitterly on trail and fever matters. W. W. Turney, a Big Bend rancher and El Paso attorney, took office as president in 1903. He called a session of all

Western rangemen at Denver, and the whole cow country got together in opposing the railroads. These cowmen of the West—staunchly united for the first time—decided that influential Murdo Mackenzie and fulminating Sam Cowan, attorney for the Texas Association, were the men to lead the attack. And off they went to Washington. There their first call was on President Roosevelt, who agreed that the Interstate Commerce Commission should have authority to fix rail rates, though he advised them that a law authorizing such power would have to be passed. At the President's suggestion, Mackenzie and Cowan went to see the Congressional Committee on Interstate and Foreign Commerce.

With their big hats covering the floor beside their chairs, Mackenzie and Cowan sat outside the committee room for ten days, virtually unnoticed except to be stared at by people rushing along the corridors.

Thinking that this was a reasonable length of time for taxpayers to warm chairs outside a public office, the Texans decided the palavering had lasted long enough. That night they telephoned ranchmen all over the West, asking them to exert all the pressure they could.

Next day they returned to their well-warmed chairs, and there they impatiently sat four more days; then magically they were invited in. This invitation, they learned, came as a result of numberless telegrams and telephone calls from all over the West. The committeemen saw that the rangemen were a solid block standing together and that they had determination in their wind-weathered eyes. The legislative mills began to grind.

The cowmen won their rate case before the Interstate Commerce Commission but then lost it in the courts, and in 1904 Murdo Mackenzie was back in the White House with a powerful suggestion—that Roosevelt include in his campaign platform a plank favoring government regulation of inter-state utilities and freight rates.

Roosevelt again agreed. He was re-elected and helped push such a bill through Congress. Of course, the railroads headed for the courthouse. Sam Cowan, who with the help of W. W. Turney, had actually authored the main provisions of the law —the Hepburn Bill—teamed up with the United States Attorney General in battling the case in the courts. At long last, the law was ruled constitutional by the United States Supreme Court.

The range cowmen had fought hard every step of the way and they had won.

After the successful siege in court the cowmen's case went back to the Interstate Commerce Commission, which not only refused the 1903 railroad rate increase but held that the cattle shippers could collect for overcharges the rails had made during the controversy.

The affected shippers assigned their claims for refunds to the Association, and suits for recovery of the overcharges were brought. The processes were slow, but finally in 1916 the cowmen received a federal court decision ordering the rails to refund $200,000 to the overcharged and now vindicated shippers.

Not only did this fight give the one-time trail drivers a victory over the railroads; it changed the basic concept of the government's right and authority to regulate.

· 15 ·

Trust Busters

Not convinced that their bouts with Texas fever on the home pasture and with the railroads in Washington were sufficient to right all their wrongs, the Davids of the cow country took on a Goliath; they tied into the big packers. There had been spasmodic sniping since the hard year when A. P. Bush's cook explained that the "taller was ransom."

The first effort of the Texas cowmen to back competition against the big packers eventually brought some of the "big five" into Texas as operators. The Yankee, Greenleaf Whittier Simpson, had put up his refrigeration plant at Fort Worth, as he had bargained to do in 1893, and he ran it successfully until 1901. Then Swift and Armour moved into Fort Worth and built major plants, and Simpson decided to go back to Boston. However, living as neighbors with the big packing houses didn't boost the market or improve relationships.

Lawyers Turney and Cowan studied the legal angles, and the cowmen charged the big packers with violation of the antitrust laws. Again the Texans were joined by their neighbors in the West in a knock-down-and-drag-out war. Up to that time there had never been a really successful national organization of livestock people, but the rate fight showed what the stockmen could accomplish on national issues by sticking together. They, therefore, ended the era of competitive "national associations" that had existed ever since the St. Louis session of 1884. On January 30, 1906, the stockmen merged the American Stock Growers Association and the National Live Stock Association. Out of this merger came the American National Live Stock Association—now the American National Cattlemen's Association—which has been a power in national policies affecting farming and ranching ever since that January day.

With hands and purposes thus joined, the cowmen set up a marketing committee to press the charges against the packers. They stirred up the press and the roast-carving public, and "Beef Trust" and "big five" became ugly phrases. Hearing the rumble from the range, President Taft promised an investigation but his term as chief executive ended before anything was accomplished. However, his successor, President Wilson, requested the Federal Trade Commission to study the question. Within a year the Commission published some astonishing figures that conclusively validated the cowmen's charges.

No British capitalist or American cow-poke had ever dreamed of a setup like it. The Trade Commission report to the President claimed that the big five jointly or separately held controlling interest in 574 companies, minority interest in ninety-five others, and undetermined interest in still another ninety-three—a total of 762 concerns—and that they produced or dealt in 775 commodities, largely food products.

The Commission report, which made big headlines over the country, stated:

In addition to meat foods, they [the packers] produce or deal in such divers commodities as fresh tomatoes and banjo strings, leather, cottonseed oil, breakfast foods, curled hair, pepsin and washing powders. Their branch houses are not only stations for distribution of meat and poultry, but take on the character of wholesale grocery stores, dealers in various kinds of produce and jobbers to special lines of trade.

They have interests large enough to be a dominating influence in most of the services connected with the production and distribution of animal foods and their byproducts, and are reaching out for control not only of substitutes of animal foods, but of substitutes for other lines into which the integration of their business has led them.

They are factors in cattle loan companies, making the necessary loans to growers and feeders of live stock; are interested in railways and private car lines transporting live stock and manu-

factured animal products, in most of the important stock yards
companies, the public market for the bulk of food animals and in
live-stock trade papers on which growers and feeders rely for
market news.

They are interested in banks from which their competitor
packing houses borrow money; in companies supplying ma-
chinery, ice, salt, materials, boxes, etc., to themselves and their
competitors; they are principal dealers on the provision ex-
changes where future prices in standard cured animal products
are determined; they or their subsidiary companies deal in hides,

oleo, fertilizer material and other crude animal byproducts. . . . Their vast distributing system, with the advantages arising from the control of private cars, cold storage and a network of branch houses, has enabled them to extend their activities on a large scale into poultry, eggs, cheese, butter, rice, breakfast foods, canned vegetables, soda fountain supplies. . . .

Charged with violating antitrust laws, the big five—Swift, Armour, Morris, Wilson and Cudahy—entered the famed Consent Decree of 1920. Under this agreement, the government would drop prosecution under the Sherman Antitrust Act and the packers would within two years get out of all lines of business except meat packing and closely allied lines "and operate under the shadow of United States courts."

The cowboys again had won, but bygones became bygones. In later years when chain supermarkets grew up and conditions developed that put the packers in a squeeze, the Southwestern cowmen were the first to petition the United States court to ease some of the conditions of the Consent Decree, which, with very few modifications, remains in effect today.

· 16 ·

Home on the Range

Of course, all the cowmen were not in Washington, huddled in conference rooms or occupying hard benches in federal courthouses; neither did they spend their full time out guarding dipping vats or searching behind every bush or clump of cactus for a rustler. They lived much like other people—maybe a little more hopefully than some, since their way through valleys of despair and hard times usually led to hills of joy and prosperity.

"The cowman is the most optimistic creature on earth," Congressman C. B. Hudspeth of Texas said in the House of Representatives. "You may bend him in every direction, but he seldom breaks; or, to use the vernacular of that section, 'loses his head.' Under his broad-brimmed Stetson hat he whistles 'Dixie' as he rides away in the morning. And about her daily affairs his helpmate sings 'How Firm a Foundation, ye saints of the Lord, is laid for your faith in His excellent word.'

"Although at that moment the roof over their heads may be sagging from the weight of a mortgage due in thirty days and no visible means of meeting it."

This art of the Westerner for being optimistic and poking fun at himself was really roped, tied and branded by a sandy-haired, lop-sidedly grinning cowboy named Will Rogers. Will grew up in Oklahoma not far from the Texas boundary;

he was part Cherokee and proud of his Indian blood. His father was a well-to-do rancher and sent his son to various schools, for he wanted him to make something of himself. Will did not take to schooling, however, explaining that after he had gone to a school for a month or two, "the teachers wouldn't seem to be running the school right, and rather than have the school stop I would generally leave." He said he spent ten years studying McGuffey's *Fourth Reader*, and at the end of that time knew more about it than McGuffey did.

While he was at Kemper Military Academy in Booneville, Missouri, Will's pal was Frank Ewing.

"When a fellow ain't got much mind, it don't take him long to make it up," the young man said, and he made up his to come back home and be a cowboy on the Ewing Ranch near Higgins, Texas, just a few miles from the Oklahoma boundary.

The range young Will rode was flat prairie broken only by a few jagged hills rimming the banks of cottonwood-bordered streams that rolled easily along until they emptied into the treacherous Canadian River. One cold autumn day when the yellow leaves were clattering away in a stiff north-western wind, Will was riding fence lines when one of his molars starting aching. Every time he opened his mouth to yell out his agony or talk to his horse, the cold air would rush in and remove the top of his head, he said. He was trying to stick out his day's work and not show up early at the bunkhouse with nothing wrong but a sore tooth when he saw Doc Rudolph Goettsche in his buckboard angling across the range toward a gate in the fence. Forgetting all about the cold air, Will yelled with all his might and galloped up to the dentist, who carried the tools of his trade with him in a little black bag as he rode from one small community to another.

"Doc, I've got the doggonedest toothache. Would you yank it out?" Will said.

"Glad to, son," the unperturbed Doc said. "Get down and stick your ugly face between the spokes of that right hind wheel."

Will got down on his knees and wedged in his aching jaw. The Doc knelt on the other side of the wheel and yanked out the tooth.

One payday on the Ewing Ranch, Will was offered money or heifers, whichever he preferred. With the typical cow-poke's longing for ownership, he decided to take the heifers. Will lived in a dugout with a cur dog as a companion. At night the dog chased coyotes if there were just a few of them, but if there were too many, the coyotes chased the dog. One wintry night there were too many coyotes, and the dog dashed, howling, into the dugout. It skidded across the floor almost into the fireplace, knocking over an andiron. The falling iron made a clear impression in the ashes. Will liked this design and adopted it as his brand. This is the way his famed Dog Iron brand came to be. It was first burned in the hide of the heifers he took from Ewing in lieu of wages.

In Fort Worth there is a coliseum almost as big as anything in Texas, where every spring cattlemen from all the cow country gather to parade their fine stock at the Southwestern Exposition and Fat Stock Show—an event started by the Cattle Raisers Association to promote better livestock and to encourage boys and girls in 4-H Club and Future Farmer activities. The building is named The Will Rogers Memorial Coliseum.

Many ranching parents, like Will's, who received their education in the college of hard knocks wanted their children to have good schooling. Phebe K. Warner, a west Texas schoolteacher, backed a "Cow-lot to College" plan for Texas youngsters:

Here is what we would like to see every ranchman and farmer do. The very day the first child is born, brand one cow or one colt or one pig for that child's educational fund. We know a girl who is building up a bunch of cattle for her college education. Her father died and left just a little property to the child and her mother. But the mother and child are raising her college fund. They have a few cows for that particular purpose. And by the time the girl is old enough to go to college the annual increase will keep the child in school and leave the little herd to depend on when the girl is through college. We know another girl who is staying out of college this year and working to save her cattle for a year at Columbia.

We know one ranchman whose only little boy owns just one fine registered heifer today. That little boy began with his pennies and dimes and what he could earn one way and another. In a few years he had a small bunch of common cattle. The father is a breeder of registered cattle. He traded and sold the boy's stock until the boy is the sole owner of the registered heifer. This little fellow is in the fifth grade now. Do you not think his cow will put him through college without a cent of help from his father except the guiding of his boy in business? Any father ought to do that for his boy.

After college, it was back to the saddle, and the age-old calling of cattle raising began profiting from the new methods of feeding and breeding that the boys had learned in the four years they had been away. However, some things were still best taught by a father.

One night Oscar Thompson, who had a border-land ranch near Hebbronville, Texas, leaned his left elbow on the dining room table and wrote some instructions to his son, Webster, who was leaving at sunup next morning with ten *vaqueros* for the East Ranch to help deliver twenty-five thousand head of cattle at Hebbronville and load them on railroad cars for shipment. The advice read:

First of all, obey orders from your boss. He is paying you for your service.

When you camp at night always point your wagon tongue toward the North Star.

Explain to your men in a quiet voice what they are to do. Don't holler at your men.

Never say "no" to your employer.

Be ready at all times to go.

When cutting cattle, cut them downhill with your back to the sun.

Don't say, "You boys do this," but, "*Come on, boys,* follow me."

Don't leave your herd for anything.

Put your two best men on the point and explain to them that they must keep the herd moving toward shipping pens.

When you graze your herd, explain to your men that they must graze toward the shipping pens or to where you are going to camp.

Water your cattle and fill them up before night.

Explain to your *cook* that he *must be ready* with his meals at all times.

Watch your horses; don't let the men abuse them.

Keep your harness and camp equipment clean and up out of the sand.

Don't fight your men unless they jump on you; but if one of them, or anyone else, jumps on you, give him the best you have.

Don't ever misrepresent anything to your employer; tell it just like it happened.

Don't get rattled. No matter what happens, keep your head clear.

Don't lose confidence in yourself; don't drink anything while on duty, and don't allow any gambling in camp.

Look after the comfort of your men and they will follow you to h—ll. Keep your mind on your business and make your head save your heels.

YOUR DAD.

In the long years of the cattle trade in the Southwest, more real wealth had come from the acquisition of property, although it might be mortgaged at first, than from cattle. Those who bought vast acreages when the price was low were fortified against economic dips and also equipped to take care of their children and grandchildren. There was a sort of equation that seemed to work out by natural law. A large ranch with common cattle grew more valuable over the years because of the great increase in the demand for land. And then, on a smaller ranch, W. C. Dibrell showed what an early investment in blue-ribbon cattle could do.

At about the time Lee Bivins moved into the Texas Panhandle, bought the famous LX outfit and became one of the nation's biggest cowmen, Mr. Dibrell, who lived on the droughty mesquite prairies of middle Texas, bought one cow named Breeze and one bull called Bangor.

Dibrell had gone to the State Fair in Dallas, looked over the Herefords, liked them and purchased Breeze and Bangor for $100 each. Without ever buying another female he became one of the major pure-bred Hereford breeders. After thirty-two years, the Dibrell family did some figuring and found that Breeze and her offspring had brought in $270,400. The appreciative family put up a marble shaft at the grave of the profitably prolific Breeze.

Men like Bivins and Dibrell were long-range planners as was old-timer C. C. Slaughter. He made a trip to thickly populated Baltimore as a delegate to the Baptist General Convention, and he took time while there to preach the gospel of the cow business. He knew that a good everyday

— HDBugbee —

demand for beef would keep the hills of joy high and wide and make those valleys shrink.

"There is no other meat like the flesh of the steer," he was quoted in *The Baltimore Sun*. "A man can eat it 365 days out of the year, and it is a brain producer. The farm laborer can consume pork products to advantage, but you city people, who live on your brains, must have beef."

Like the Dibrell family's sticking with one breed, the Cattle Raisers Association kept its line of succession. In 1910, Berkley Spiller, a grandson of old Jim Loving, took over the job of secretary-manager and chief-in-charge of rustler chasers. Spiller had been working in the office since the death of Loving.

New men growing up on the range possessed, or inherited, a famed characteristic of the old—the ability to co-operate with the inevitable.

Soon after Jim Callan took over the presidency of the Association in 1909, he bought a herd of sheep. "I heard W. A. Glasscock say that in his country around Sonora the sheepmen were staying in hotels and the cowmen in the wagonyard," Callan said, "and I decided I wanted to be prepared if such sentiment strikes the whole country.

"I really am not sure that I can tell a ewe from a ram, and I told the man I bought my sheep from just to ship them to me before I saw them. He insisted, however, on showing them to me; so I went out to his ranch and looked wise and told him they were just what I wanted."

The fact that the head of Cattle Raisers was also a sheep owner didn't raise any eyebrows, for Texas cowmen never developed a violent animosity for the woolly animals. However, at this time the nation's last great range war, a battle between cowmen and sheep growers, raged in Wyoming.

With the Texans the idea was to make a living out of land and livestock, whether the stock were long or short of horn or mooed, baaed or gave milk. Ed C. Lasater, who followed Callan as head of the cowmen, was reared on a sheep ranch. On his Rio Grande Valley spread, which was a few acres bigger than Rhode Island, he established one of the nation's largest dairies. While making a success of his milk and cream project, Lasater had a strange, hump-shouldered breed of cattle in his beef herd.

Al McFaddin, with the Brahman bull he had bought from the Hagenbach Circus in St. Louis, and A. P. Borden, with the sacred cows he had imported from India, had changed the looks of cattle in the coastal country. The Brahman breed proved exceptionally profitable for that low-altitude, hot-summered country.

McFaddin, who took office as president in 1912, was the first Brahman breeder to head the cowmen. The McFaddins were pioneers in other ways. The family had moved to Texas from Tennessee in 1817, which was five years before the first official colonists under Moses and Stephen F. Austin got there. McFaddin was the first Texas cowman to get rich in oil; he got into that lucrative sideline in 1903 when the great Spindletop field at Beaumont gushed forth.

Honoring Texas' leading hero, McFaddin named one of his best Brahman bulls Sam Houston.

Robert J. Kleberg, Sr., of the King Ranch, liked the way the Brahmans adapted themselves to the climate and produced beef. With a half-breed Shorthorn-Brahman bull given the ranch by Tom O'Connor and cattle later brought from Borden, Kleberg started experiments which led to the first breed of cattle developed in North America—the big, cherry-red Santa Gertrudis of the King Ranch.

While the southern Texans were getting their Brahmans

established, cowmen all over the Southwest were likewise ranching with heavier, beefier breeds than the old longhorn —Herefords, Shorthorns, Aberdeen-Angus. Out in the Big Bend country, where the spires of the Chisos Mountains rise, the Hereford was becoming king. The first ranchers in that wide land, which the plowing settlers have never liked, had to fortify their places against the raids of border bandits. One of them, Lawrence Haley, fortified his against women, there being a stern edict that no woman would be permitted on his ranch. Haley willed his ranch to his cowboys—provided that they would put over his grave a tombstone bearing the carved likeness of a cow, a horse and a sheep. The stone stands today near Alpine.

Early Big Bend ranchers—like W. B. Mitchell and L. C. Brite—started breeding Herefords of the sort that Corn Belt feeders liked to buy for their lots. Out of this work came the famous Highland Hereford, which is considered one of the best feeder animals in the nation.

Frank Hastings, manager of Swenson Ranch in western Texas, likewise bred Herefords to suit the feeders. He was so successful at this that the Swenson outfit developed the first big mail-order business for feeder stock; the feeders simply wrote in their orders without ever seeing what they were buying.

Collecting cow horns was an old Western custom, and about this time, the world-famous collection of horns that had long decorated the old Buckhorn Saloon in San Antonio was sold to a collector in Cuba for $90,000. In the group were the head and horns of an African antelope which Theodore Roosevelt gave the Buckhorn when he was in San Antonio organizing his Rough Riders. However, some of the prize sets of horns with fabulous spreads were from the heads of old-time Texas longhorn steers.

The hefty bovines out on the range could have used those horns to ward off shaggy lobo wolves, mountain lions and enormous wildcats. In breeding beef quality into their cattle, the ranchers also bred out some qualities—the ferocious fighting spirit and agility of the self-reliant longhorn. Somewhere in this planned breeding program, the balance of nature was tipped, and the ranchmen, who hadn't considered that factor, now had to fight predators.

As early as the 1890's, they suffered heavy losses from wild animals, and nearly all of the men in the Association paid bounties up to $50 for each lobo killed. But the predators, flourishing on highly bred beef, increased so rapidly that the state, at the insistence of the cowmen, had to join in offering rewards. A good many cowpunchers shifted professions and became wolfers, and hunters took to the range to harvest that bounty money.

In the two-year period ending in April, 1914, the State of Texas paid bounties on 8,592 lobos, 68,627 coyotes, 21,665 wildcats, ten Mexican lions, fifty-three panthers and twenty-two leopard cats. Then the United States Bureau of Biological Survey joined the fight, and the hungry predators were finally controlled. (In 1954, after reading this report on the killing of lobo wolves, Joe Reynolds of Fort Worth, who ranches on a major scale in the Big Bend country, remarked, "There weren't that many lobos in 1914. The state probably paid on that many, but the state probably paid on a lot of big coyotes which the hunters claimed were lobos.")

However, the four-legged beasts never stirred the cowmen like the "two-legged coyotes." By 1913, Mexico seethed with revolutionary violence. Border bandits took advantage of the isolation of the Big Bend to steal cattle and otherwise plunder the ranches. On February 9 of that year, Association Inspector J. A. Harvick and two United States river guards on the Rio Grande, Jack Howard and Joe Sitter, captured Chico Cana, a suspected cow thief, and started toward the town of Valentine with him. On the way, over a mountain trail, the officers rode into an ambush.

Volleys of rifle fire crackled from behind rocks. Howard was killed and Sitter and Inspector Harvick were wounded. Cana escaped. Harvick reported that Lina Baiza, the leader of a gang of border bandits, had set up the ambush to free his lieutenant.

A year later, the Association's chief field inspector, John R. Banister, was dispatched to the Big Bend with instructions to end the Baiza raids. Banister found Sheriff M. B. Chastain of Presidio County (also an Association inspector) and River Guards Sitter, Charles Craighead and Sam Neal ready to ride the border in search of Baiza. Banister joined them.

Four days later the men were deep in the mountain gulches along the Rio. Riding into a Mexican village, on the Texas side of the river, they saw a man dash from a hut, leap on a horse and hit the breeze for the Rio some fifty yards away.

Sitter spurred his horse to the door of a hut and asked the identity of the man.

"Lina Baiza," a large-eyed Mexican woman said.

The men jumped off their mounts and opened fire. The running horse tumbled into the river near the point of a small island that was covered with driftwood. The man clambered off the horse and crawled into a drift.

Inspector Banister told of the action in his report to the Fort Worth office:

Sheriff Chastain mounted his horse and said, "Boys, let's go to him." Another of the party and I mounted and with Mr. Chastain rode across to the island, dismounted and approached the drift in which the fugitive had taken shelter. We could not see Baiza until we were within a few feet of the drift, and when discovered he was seen to adjust himself toward us and prepare to shoot, and he was killed. . . . I heard the river guards on the bank yell for us to get away.

Almost instantly we were fired upon by members of Baiza's band from the Mexican side.

. . . We have since been informed that Chico Cana, the other leader of this notorious band of outlaws, was captured.

This was the start of a siege of border trouble, first by the bandits and then by the men of Pancho Villa. Nearly every ranch along the border was plundered, and herds of cattle and goats were driven into Mexico. During the years of the worst of the raids, a one-time trail driver and Texas Ranger, Joe D. Jackson, was president of Texas Cattle Raisers. His ranch in the Big Bend was not far from the border. Realizing the danger lurking there, Jackson deployed a majority of the Association inspectors to that region. They teamed up with Texas Rangers, sheriffs and United States Customs agents to protect American property.

But the conflict grew and the United States government recognized its international proportions. The Army was sent to take over.

Then in April, 1917, Uncle Sam's doughboys had other borders to defend.

The first desperate words that reached the cowmen when war broke out in Europe were "cattle shortage" and "beef scarcity." Except for a cow-killing cold winter in 1917 and a destructive drought in 1918, the war years brought the cattle business a booming rise in market values, for meat was needed to feed fighting men here and abroad. Often civilians had meatless days so that the quantities needed by the Army would be available.

Winning the war was now the big job on hand. At the March, 1918, convention in Dallas, the cowmen said:

... We stand unqualifiedly with President Wilson and those charged with the conduct of the war and administration of the country's affairs, believing ... that in reasonable time they will lead us to a KAISER FUNERAL and a DEMOCRATIC PEACE.

One of the loud "amens" came from C. C. Slaughter, who was leaning on crutches. Some time before, he had fallen and injured his hip.

There were many men present who prayed that peace would come soon, for their sons, cowboys and farm boys were among the thousands of volunteers who donned khaki leggings and rode with the Yanks the rough, submarine-infested waters of the Atlantic Ocean to fight "over there." Across the prairies and wooded hills, lonesome homes proudly displayed in windows closest to the roads little flags bearing stars.

Fathers left at home rode and worked from before dawn until after dark taking care of the cattle, so that when the boys came home there would be a good herd and the home range for them to help the "old man" operate.

Shortage of labor in the cattle country grew acute for the first time in its history. One hard-working rancher, Carl E. Sams of the Anchor D in New Mexico, was inspired to practical poetry:

Sears and Roebuck, Chicago, Illinois, I am in need of three well-equipped cowboys, so send in that number by parcel post. I am not particular, just anything most.

Dayton Moses, who had succeeded Sam Cowan as the Association attorney, had three sons in the armed forces; he and the far-flung Association inspectors worked overtime, as did the ranchers. Not even war stopped the ever-necessary pursuit of the violators of the Eighth Commandment—one department of the cattle business where there never seemed to be a shortage.

"It is unfortunately true," Moses reported in October 1918, "that cattle stealing is on the increase, occasioned no doubt by the fact that nearly all of the experienced help on the cattle ranches have gone to war, leaving the range unprotected and the cattle in the care of inexperienced and incompetent ranch help. It is believed that there would have been many more cases of cattle theft reported had it not been for the severe drought in a large portion of the range, and the members are advised to watch their herds carefully this fall and winter.

"On account of the prevalence of Spanish influenza and the Liberty Loan Drive, but few courts have been in session during October where cattle-theft cases are pending."

Soon after the ending of World War I, the exit time came for an old actor in the cattlelands drama. Early in 1919, the first native-born son of the Texas Republic and champion war horse of the cowmen, C. C. Slaughter, died—the last of the three bewhiskered horsemen who had saddled up that dawn and jogged across Dillingham Prairie to the raw little village of Graham, where they banded together forty honest men to stand against the thieves.

The Texas and Southwestern

The air was fresh over the sun-washed and wind-swept grazing lands when the boys came home from service. Men hopefully harbored the thought that "the war fought to end wars" was now over, that everyone could settle down to the business of just living and amounting to something. It might even be that the time of the seven fat years was at hand—as Joseph had once promised Egyptian cattlemen. The price of cattle was holding up so that there was a feeling of prosperity all over the cow country. From their ranges, cowmen had been told, would have to come the cows and bulls to restock the war-ravaged fields of Europe.

The boys studying stock-raising at Texas A. & M. College had a two-year-old steer named Marshal Foch. There was wild celebration when he was named the grand champion steer at the Southwestern Exposition and Fat Stock Show at Fort Worth. Another Angus, General Pershing, was the champion yearling steer.

However, the comforts of the new-won peace and prosperity were short-lived. The postwar boom of inflationary 1919 broke almost overnight, and nearly every rancher in the cow country was knocked downhill. During the war cattlemen had borrowed to the hilt in order to increase their production so that they could help feed the world. The banks were likewise caught; they demanded quick liquidation of herds before the market plunged to rock bottom. This rush to market, of course, sent prices plunging downward. It was the valley again—the nation's cowmen saw their industry flat and broke. Within a year the range country had only fifty per cent of the normal population of beef cattle, and even the value of the byproducts sank to an all-time low.

In 1920 a bull on the ranch of J. T. Davis near Sterling, Texas, died—perhaps from loneliness. Davis told one of his cowboys that if he would remove the hide and sell it he could have part of the money to buy some bridle reins. After bargaining in town for half a day the cowboy managed to sell the hide for $1.55. He bought his bridle reins, which cost $1.50, and took Davis his nickel change.

A little later, Lee Bivins was trying desperately to get a thousand steers from his Panhandle ranch to market. A widespread strike of railroad shopmen had crippled transportation at a time when nearly every rancher in the West was heading for the stockyards.

One day the railroad agent in Amarillo told Bivins that if he could get his steers into town within a few hours there would be cars for them. Looking at his watch and calculating for a moment, Bivins saw that he couldn't make the three-hour trip to the ranch by car and then get the steers trucked to town in time to claim the railroad cars.

Thereupon, he rented an airplane and a barnstorming pilot and sent a knee-shaking puncher roaring to the ranch with orders for his men to get the steers to town.

"Just imagine," Bivins told a friend, "it took only thirty-two minutes for that airplane to get out to the ranch."

The steers made the deadline and rolled away, with Bivins hoping they reached Kansas City before another drop in price.

Ike Pryor and W. W. Turney pleaded with the large ranchers to pay off their notes at the banks so that the loans which had been made to the smaller operators, who had no resources for paying debts other than their cattle, could be carried longer. John Clay had weathered the blizzard and bust of 1886-87 in Wyoming where the snow fell deepest. He made speeches throughout the Southwest and wrote pieces for the stock journals, saying, "Keep a stiff upper lip! After the debacle of the 1880's we found our money where we lost it, and we'll do this again."

Out in the Big Bend, John Young, a newer prophet of the cattlelands, wrote in *The Alpine Avalanche:*

"No real cowman will ever be broke until his neck is broken, as they are made of sterner stuff; you cannot keep a squirrel on the ground."

"This is a time for sober thought and sane business; for less jazz and joyriding and more work," advised the cowmen's own magazine, *The Cattleman.*

Just as their forebears had done when the going got rough, the younger ranchers drew together. The Panhandle and Southwestern Live Stock Association, the organization Goodnight had set up to protect the Panhandle during the days of the trail fight, had held on and it had a substantial membership in western Texas and New Mexico. In 1921, the Texas Cattle Raisers and the Panhandle groups consolidated and became the Texas and Southwestern Cattle Raisers Association.

The bounds of the members in the band started under the spreading oak now stretched far over the horizons that the pioneers kept following. There were members all over Texas and in Kansas, New Mexico, Oklahoma, Arizona, Arkansas, California, Colorado, Florida, Haiti, the Republic of Mexico, Illinois, Iowa, Louisiana, Michigan, Missouri, Montana, New

York, Utah, Virginia, West Virginia and Wyoming. The majority of the members were in Texas.

The old outfit with the new name retained a veteran as their president—W. W. Turney, who had first been president of Texas Cattle Raisers back in 1903-06.

The background was broader, but the Texas and Southwestern still faced that familiar contingency that the forty men at Graham had known so well. Because of the cussedness of men and economic forces as well, the rustlers kept their range broad, also, and were as active as ever. However, now only the ignorant, desperate or very daring rustler would steal Association cows because he knew that somewhere along the line an inspector would pop up and ask, "How about this?"

On a June day in 1921 a man who had a small ranch near Perryton in the Texas Panhandle asked the railroad agent to have a stock car ready within one week. That night he drove his truck onto the ranch of Mrs. Sherman Jines, loaded nineteen cattle and hauled them to his pasture. The next night in a general foray he picked up cattle belonging to H. C. Dodson, Wilkerson and Son and A. L. Dowers and took nine more head to his pasture. Mrs. Jines was the only one in the group who belonged to the Texas and Southwestern.

Late on a Sunday evening the rustler moved his stolen herd to the railroad. He drove all night, loaded his car and started the cattle off to Kansas City.

Texas and Southwestern Inspectors Calohan and McCoy were out in the Kansas City yards inspecting brands on all the cattle that came in. They noticed Mrs. Jines's cattle and got in touch with her. This was the first Mrs. Jines knew that she had lost any stock. She recovered her cattle and so did all the nonmembers whose stock were in that shipment.

A few days later the man was picked up and jailed on charges of cattle theft. He told inspectors that he owed a bank $350 and that the bank had been on his tail; he had decided that the easiest way to meet an honest debt was to steal a carload of cattle. "I didn't know Mrs. Jines belonged to the Texas and Southwestern," he remarked.

The day of mechanized rustling had come. A thief could drive onto a ranch after dark, load a few calves and by driving all night be three hundred miles from the scene by the next day. Such truck-riding rustlers usually slaughtered the stolen beef and sold to unscrupulous "fence" retail markets. The range was too wide to be lighted at night or to be protected like property in town with a police force. Only the small band of inspectors were on guard in the expanded world of the Texas and Southwestern.

On the evening of Easter in 1923, Inspectors H. L. Roberson and Dave Allison chatted with half-a-dozen men in the dimly lighted lobby of the little Gaines Hotel in Seminole, Texas, out near the New Mexico line. Mrs. Roberson had gone upstairs to bed. Among the men talking with the inspectors were the sheriff of the county and the district attorney.

Roberson and Allison were there to testify before the grand jury against Milt Good and Tom Ross, who had been charged with cattle theft in Texas and New Mexico. While working in that area the inspectors had taken charge of some six hundred stolen cattle.

A few moments after Mrs. Roberson left the lobby, two men eased in at the front door and opened up with shotgun and pistols. Twenty shots roared out, breaking the Easter calm.

Roberson and Allison were cut to pieces with bullets and shotgun charges. No one else in the lobby was hit.

Mrs. Roberson ran downstairs. Seeing that her husband was dead, she grabbed his .45 caliber automatic. But the handle had been shattered by bullets, and then Mrs. Roberson grabbed a small-caliber pistol which Roberson carried under his belt. She ran out of the hotel and along a street behind two fleeing men. When they stopped at an automobile she opened fire. One of her bullets hit a belt buckle and caused only a slight wound. She shot the other man in the arm and the bullet lodged in his hip.

Later in the night Ross and Good surrendered.

They claimed they had shot in self-defense, that the inspectors had threatened their lives.

Tall, dignified Cyrus Lucas was then president of the Texas and Southwestern, one of the most scholarly men ever to head it. He was a student of Shakespeare and loved fine music and poetry. He didn't smoke or drink; his cowmen friends said he looked and acted like a king.

Lucas lost no time in going into action. First he wrote all the members suggesting that each contribute to a fund for the widows of the slain inspectors. Five thousand dollars rolled in within a week. Then Lucas wrote the members telling of definite steps he had taken:

The lawless element of western Texas and eastern New Mexico were very much mistaken if they thought that by the murder of these two men they would destroy by intimidation the activities of this Association. Hardly had the news gone forth that this crime was committed before Inspectors Hawkins from Marfa, Chesher from Hereford, Davis from Paducah, Southworth from Dickens, Hogan from Fort Worth and former Inspector Harvick from Ozona moved into that section, quietly but effectively by their presence letting the bad element know that Roberson and Allison belonged to a body of men who know no fear and shirk no duty. . . .

The cowmen voted to pay Mrs. Roberson and Mrs. Allison $50 a month each for life.

Good and Ross were convicted and given long prison terms. Later they escaped from the Texas penitentiary. Ross was found shot to death in Montana. Good was recaptured in Oklahoma. Several years later he was given a gubernatorial pardon; then he wrote a book about his side of the case.

If modern rustlers could become daring and ride in swift machines, so could the Scotland Yard of the cow country. Everything about the inspection and detective system was tightened, made more efficient. Some thirty field inspectors rode the range and were subject to call by any member who lost cattle or observed suspicious characters about his place. Wherever there was any important movement of cattle, at least one field inspector was on hand to check the brands.

The rustler who managed to get by these range detectives with stolen stuff had still another big hurdle to cross. Market inspectors were on hand at nearly all the major markets—Denver, Oklahoma City, the National Stock Yards in Illinois, Fort Worth, San Antonio, St. Joseph, Missouri, Kansas City, to name only a few. These men took a look at all the incoming cattle, often having to clip hair off their sides or rumps in order clearly to see the marks, and recorded all the brands. When Association cows hit the markets, the inspectors determined quickly whether the rightful owners had shipped them. If there was any doubt about this, the inspectors cut out the cattle and held them. If the cattle had been stolen, the cattle were held for the owner, and the inspectors started tracing back to see how these Association beeves happened to get away from their home range. Somewhere along the line, there was bound to be a rustler.

This hurdle was not the final difficulty for the rustler, however. As soon as a man was suspected as a thief, the Association's legal force joined the hunt, helped work up evidence and then went into the courthouse and aided the district attorney in prosecuting the offender.

Moreover, the inspectors kept their eyes peeled for unlawful or "fence" butcher shops. Around such places, and almost everywhere, they searched for cowhides bearing telltale brands; always the toughest job of the thief was disposing of the hide so that it could never be found.

This was a small police force for such an enormous range area—and they had to know thousands of brands—but the men whose life work was tracking down thieves were so keenly trained and had so much experience that they could almost smell a cattle rustler two hundred and fifty yards away.

Once at Lubbock, Texas, Bill Luman, long a field inspector in the Texas Panhandle, saw a truckload of steers that bore an obscure brand. He asked where the animals came from, and was told that they had been raised on a nearby stock farm.

"Don't believe it!" Luman snorted. "Look at those flinty little hoofs. Those steers came from where there are mountains and rocks."

Luman couldn't resist the urge to investigate. Starting with only the one clue, he back-tracked, picking up bits of information here and there. Months later he broke a big rustling case. The steers had been stolen as unbranded calves from Association members in the mountainous Big Bend country. Luman's work broke up a gang of motorized calf stealers and sent three men to prison.

Graves Peeler—deafened in one ear by a rustler's bullet that nicked it—became a legendary rustler chaser in the West. Inspectors got wind of a gang suspected of stealing Texas cattle and hauling them to Arizona. During the winter Peeler was sent to Arizona on the case. He traveled the mountains where the snow was so deep and tightly packed that he could ride his horse over fences. By keen observation, he found that a good-sized herd had been moved from the snowy mountains to hidden valleys with socks and pieces of tow sacking tied over the feet of the cattle so that they made no clear tracks. Peeler figured that only rustlers would do that.

In a valley he spotted stolen cattle and a camp. He rode into the camp that night and said, "I'm hungry as hell. You cow thieves fix me some grub. I'm spending the night with you, and in the morning we go to jail."

And that's what happened.

Despite the variety of other problems that beset range cowmen, the Association paid strict attention to its job of fighting thieves. It hired vigorous, adventurous young men to join the ranks of old-timers like Graves Peeler—a breed of men who just naturally liked to chase cattle rustlers for a living.

When the Texas and Southwestern celebrated its golden anniversary in 1926 the retiring president, H. L. Kokernot, whose family had been ranching in Texas since the days of the Republic, suggested that young blood was needed.

Ex-President Joe D. Jackson agreed. "Older men are just like old cutting horses," he said; "after years of hard work and toil these old horses will get sprung-kneed, big-ankled and sore-backed and get so stiffened up until they are dangerous to ride. We have got to get new and younger men."

And they did.

For the first time, the son of a former president became boss man; young Richard M. Kleberg of the King Ranch, son of R. J. Kleberg, Sr., was elected president. J. Malcolm

Shelton of Amarillo, son of an old-time member, John M. Shelton, was picked as first vice-president, and C. C. Slaughter, Jr., went in as second vice-president.

Only three of the old founders were able to attend this milestone event—H. G. Bedford, D. B. Gardner and J. H. Graham. With golden badges shining, they were seated on the stage with the convention celebrities—Secretary of Agriculture W. M. Jardine and Gutzon Borglum, the sculptor, who had been commissioned to design a thirty-three-foot-high memorial to the old trail drivers of Texas, the marble to be placed at the foot of the Old Chisholm Trail in San Antonio.

And the gay 1920's galloped along.

On a bright Sunday afternoon not too long after the 1929 stock market crash the people of a small ranching community in Kansas gathered in a little church for the funeral of a neighbor. Sun rays penetrating the west windows made the stained glass glow. About midway through the service, darkness enveloped the church, and no one could see the windows. The people were panicked and several of them hurried outside; out there they found that zero visibility prevailed. The air was black with velvety dust. Lights, quickly turned on, made only a dull, yellowish glow.

The Kansas community was not the only one to be stricken by midafternoon darkness. The dust storm, the first of many to sweep over the cow country, covered the prairie states from the Dakotas on the north and Colorado and New Mexico on the west; it drifted stiflingly across Oklahoma and Texas. Drought burned nearly all the country west of Ohio.

Not long after the dusters started, a stockman in the Oklahoma Panhandle reported that his cattle in nuzzling for grass roots had eaten so much dirt that they were dying. Near Dalhart, Texas, on a portion of the old XIT Ranch, crows built a nest of rusted barbed wire in a dying locust tree that stood on an abandoned farmstead; in that plains country, dotted with sharp-crested, glistening sand dunes, there was no other material for building a nest.

Farming families by the thousands in western Oklahoma loaded their belongings in, and on top of, their weathered cars and chugged westward to California. One farmer who had wrestled with the soil for twenty years said that he was droughted out so bad that all he had to do to move was put his wife and kids in the car and call the dog.

The farm folks in the westbound stream of jalopies were first known as "Okies," though all of them were not from Oklahoma; later, after John Steinbeck wrote the novel *The Grapes of Wrath*, they were known as the Joads.

In March of 1933, Dolph Briscoe of Uvalde, president of the Texas and Southwestern, went to Fort Worth to confer with Association Manager Berkley Spiller and a few cowmen he had called to meet there. This was shortly after the inauguration of Franklin D. Roosevelt as President and Briscoe's fellow townsman, John Nance Garner, as Vice-President. Telling about this Fort Worth session a little later, Briscoe said:

That was the first time in the history of the Association that it was ever seriously considered that we would not hold our convention on the stated dates. I talked with Mr. Spiller and with several other members of the Association, and we seriously considered calling off the convention . . . because of the chaotic condition of the country. . . .

In July of the same year, Briscoe was back in Fort Worth, and this time he conferred with H. L. Kokernot of the Big Bend country, G. R. White of the Texas hill country and

Tom Coble of the Panhandle. They studied a situation almost as black as any dust storm.

For them, the problem was a grave one, involving not only drought and depression and, as Briscoe said later, "the threat of riots all over the country," but the long and great tradition of the range. Out there the men had always been self-reliant, lovers of independence and elbowroom. They had braved the Indians, the outlaws, the weather, the storms and swollen rivers. Except in the case of livestock diseases, such as the Texas fever and sporadic outbursts of foot-and-mouth disease, the cowmen had never sought aid from the government.

The grave men meeting in Fort Worth, all of them descendants of frontier cattle families, telephoned friends from one end of the cow country to the other to see whether they could hear a single encouraging word. There were only reports of great gloom.

Then Briscoe telephoned F. E. Mollin, manager of the American National Cattlemen's Association in Denver; for nearly thirty years the cowmen had channeled their national problems, such as the packer fight, through the American National. In the course of the long telephone conversation, Mollin and the Texans decided to call a session of rangemen to meet in Denver the next month. Out of this two-day conference came the appointment of a committee, headed by Mollin and Briscoe, to go to Washington.

This action eventually came to a climax in the hot summer of 1934, when the biggest, strangest and most heartbreaking cattle deal of all times was made and executed—the controversial emergency buying program.

The drought-stricken stockman was the seller; the Federal Surplus Relief Corporation, the buyer. In each of twenty-three affected states a man from the Bureau of Animal Industry was the range boss, the county agents were the "foremen" and the appraisers and veterinarians were the wagon bosses. In keeping with range custom, Uncle Sam, the buyer, had to have a brand for the stock he was buying. He chose a chemical to apply it with, however, rather than a hot branding iron. The government shipped a good many of the cattle to grass in other states, and these were branded with an "R," for "relief," on the left hip. Condemned cattle were put out of their misery on the spot. Those that were eating-beef quality went to slaughter and immediately to the relief larders.

President Cleveland's forced roundup on the Arapahoe-Cheyenne range in 1885 was merely a Sunday rodeo in a cow pasture compared to the government roundup of 1934. In Texas, cattle were sold at the rate of thirty thousand a day. Every stockyard and nearly every freight train sounded with the bawling of drought cows. In the twenty-three states, the government bought eight million cattle at an average of about $13 each.

Out on the range the tears streamed down the faces of many old cowmen when they saw the government roundup —not because of the drought or the condition of the starving cattle, but because they didn't want the government "running our business." Man after man refused to sell to the government, though he had no other market.

Albert K. Mitchell, who was then managing the Big Bell Ranch in New Mexico, "ran" from the government buying program. He loaded the thousands of Bell cattle on freight trains and headed for Mexico; there he leased range and kept the cattle until grass greened again on the Bell.

However, few could do as Mitchell was able to do; for nearly every man who owned cows only one way was open —sell to the government or see his animals starve and die of thirst in the pasture—and he pridefully joined Uncle Sam's great roundup.

One day when the dust of that roundup had filled the sky in the eastern part of the Panhandle where the Texas plains join the old Cherokee Strip, Roy Sansing whistled happily as he rode up to his wind-blown ranch house near Higgins. For a year he had been keeping his family going by milking bony beef cows and selling the cream his wife, Clara, skimmed off the milk.

When he arrived home in such a happy mood, Clara asked the reason for the jubilation.

"Topped the relief market today," he said. "Sold a cow for $20, which was the very top the government paid in Lipscomb County today."

Although the old-timers who had to ride long distances on horseback to attend meetings always managed somehow to be on hand, the modern cowmen with automobiles, airplanes and fast trains didn't have the time or money to attend the numerous policy sessions during the emergency. As a result, the executive committee of the Texas and Southwestern virtually ceased to function and the affairs of the Association were left to a committee of five men—Tom Coble (who was elected president in 1934), J. C. McGill, Joe Sneed, H. L. Kokernot and Claude McCan.

However, there was wide-spread interest in the 1935 session of the Texas and Southwestern, cattle people everywhere wondering whether there would be a knock-down-and-drag-out fight over the issue of joining Uncle Sam's roundup. President Tom Coble expressed the official viewpoint and the Association approved by vote what he said:

A year ago we realized the surplus supplies would have to be disposed of before the price level could be raised. Our problem was to accomplish this, if possible, by some means other than the old process of price-destroying liquidation. . . . The result was the government cattle-buying program which was organized and put into operation very speedily. This program accomplished the saving of a large food supply which was necessary for the needy, furnished a market for cattle which could not have been found otherwise, and resulted in the removal of the surplus.

Still there were loud cries that the New Deal had taken over the cow business, that at last the rugged individuals of the range had sold their independence for money from Washington.

Nearly all the cowmen participated in the government range program that followed the drought emergency—a program of improvement and conservation conceived largely by Marvin Jones, then a Texas congressman and chairman of the House Committee on Agriculture; Grover Hill, a Texan who later was Under-Secretary of Agriculture; and Jay Taylor, a rising young cowman of Amarillo. But it wasn't long before the men of Texas and Southwestern demonstrated that they still had their independence and could disagree with the same Uncle Sam who had bought their cattle.

In fostering his Good Neighbor policy, President Roosevelt negotiated with Argentina a treaty known as the Argentina Sanitary Pact. Under it, beef from the pampas of the Argentine would be imported into the United States.

Almost as soon as this was announced, the directors of the Texas and Southwestern got together—hot under the collar—at Houston and mapped strategy to block ratification of the treaty by the United States Senate. They didn't want the competition of Argentina beef, which could be produced much more cheaply than in this country, and they said so. Moreover, they had a perfect prod pole with which to jab: the foot-and-mouth disease—even a worse pestilence than Texas fever ever proved to be—was prevalent in Argentina. The cowmen took the stand that importation of the beef would, therefore, be gravely dangerous, that an epidemic of the disease could wipe out the beef and dairy industries in the United States. Through the years the cowmen had experienced scattered outbreaks of the disease, and in each case every infected cow had had to be slaughtered and put in a lime pit. They proved by the statements of veterinarians that the importation of Argentina beef in any form could plant the disease in the United States.

The American National also opposed the pact, thereby bringing together the forces of the rangemen in strong opposition to this phase of the Good Neighbor policy. The treaty was pigeonholed in the Committee on International Affairs, and there it remained in 1954.

At this same Houston session, the Texans proposed a gigantic beef advertising program—to be financed by ranchmen. Ever since the early 1920's the National Live Stock and Meat Board in Chicago, supported by cowmen and packers, had promoted beef-eating. Back in 1929 the board had made much of a tasty experiment in New York, where two men lived a full year with nothing to eat except meat and at the end were happy, healthful and hungry for a steak. The men were Vilhjalmur Stefansson and Karsten Anderson, both famed as Arctic explorers. Tired of wandering, the men had settled in New York to do some writing, and it was Stefansson who had suggested the experiment. This project was conducted at the Russell Sage Institute of Pathology on funds from the Institute of American Meat Packers. Scientists, headed by Dr. Raymond Pearl of Johns Hopkins University, supervised it.

"They came out of it in fine shape," the Meat Board pointed out, "which may be of interest to those under the spell of the 'don't eat meat' bogies."

Now the cowmen wanted the Meat Board activity increased to "the size of cigarette advertising." Jay Taylor was appointed to take up the matter with ranchers all over the cow country. He attended their meetings and explained the plan, and they liked it sufficiently to chip in money to pay for the advertising—a trial run at first and then an all-out proposition.

This was getting off to a good start when war and rumors of war filled newspapers and magazines and came blaring forth from radios. In this uncertain time—on January 30, 1937—a strong branch connection with the old oak-tree cowmen came to an end. Association Manager Berkley Spiller died. Frank McGill, who long had been a stalwart among cowmen, was then president of the Texas and Southwestern. When he heard of the death of the grandson of Jim Loving, he wrote a statement to all the members: "The Great Master in His wisdom has called our beloved and long-time secretary and general manager," he said. "There is no doubt in my mind that He is preparing for the Great Roundup and needed Berkley's help. . . ."

Henry Bell, who had been with the Texas and Southwestern for seventeen years, took over in the home office and was handed a tough assignment. The cowmen's outfit, having come through a depression, wasn't very prosperous. Nearly all the days of its life, it had been in debt or, at best, operating on current revenues. When costly emergencies popped up, the Association usually had to gallop to the bank. Now more money was necessary. With many local problems being affected by action in Washington, it was deemed necessary to keep the Association's attorney in the capital a great deal of the time. Dayton Moses, who had prosecuted cattle rustlers for years, resigned, and Joe Montague, a big man who wears a black hat, succeeded him.

McGill, a quiet, easygoing south Texan, seldom opened his mouth except when he had something meaningful to say. He looked over the books and financial records and opened his mouth: "We've got to get this outfit out of debt and build up a backlog. We need more members. Every cattleman in the Southwest should be with us."

Thereupon, Bell was given the job of building up the organization, numerically and dollar-wise. He did it effectively in troublous times; not many years later, the membership had doubled, extending to nearly all the range states, and the prospering outfit was able to pay cash for a fine new headquarters in Fort Worth. Moreover, the Association had a reserve rich enough to carry it over a prolonged period of hard times.

As had been the case since 1877, there stretched the unknown trail ahead.

· *18* ·

Gospel of the Cow Business

No one had dreamed it could ever happen, but the great old Matador Ranch was sold and split up. This eight hundred thousand acres of Texas plains range had been owned for generations by a Scots syndicate in Dundee. The American managers, Murdo Mackenzie and later his son, John Mackenzie, had made it one of the storied beef outfits in America. It was bringing in around $1,000,000 a year at the time it was sold to nonranching New York speculators for $19,000,000 in 1950.

All the other land and cattle kingdoms which had been financed from the British Isles had already come into American ownership or long ago had been sliced up into farms. Therefore, the Matador was the last Scots syndicate ranch in Texas, if not in the Southwest. Because of this, its venerable age and its solid success, there was deep sentiment attached to the old outfit of the Flying V cattle brand and the "Fifty" horse mark. It still kept a chuck wagon rolling on the range and it had real cowboys, who could tell the time by the sun, and a *remuda* of fractious horses. Here on this stretch of rangeland the scenes and sounds and smells of the Old West remained.

To people who knew the cow country, the Matador, like the North Star, had always been there and apparently always would be.

But perplexities of recent times had led to its dissolution, and also caused a good many other things never faced by old Jim Loving or G. W. Evans, who moved far away because he had enough neighbors to consume a shoat in one day. The latest boom-and-bust period, which followed almost precisely the weather and human pattern of the 1870's and 1880's, dated approximately from the Japanese attack on Pearl Harbor.

At that time, Jay Taylor, son of a cowboy-wagon boss who made the Cherokee Strip run for a homestead, was president of the Texas and Southwestern. He was soon in the Army, and the concern then was not for advertising beef, as Taylor had advocated, but for producing enough meat for the ration points which were carefully guarded and counted by the women.

This was the job of Western rangemen, such as Claude McCan and Holman Cartwright, the other wartime heads of the old Association which had carried on through earlier conflicts. Men of the Texas and Southwestern opposed government controls of beef; so did the American National and most of the Western cowmen. They particularly objected to the practice of government agencies of changing policy overnight. It took long-range planning to produce beef animals and also to finish them on feed. For example, a feeder couldn't buy cattle and put feed in them if the government was likely to change the price structure without notice; he could lose his shirt in a hurry.

So the producer-feeder combine which had developed and worked so well—the rangeman raising the animal and the feeder, mainly in the Corn Belt, finishing it into the dining room product—broke down, and the nation depended largely on grass-fed beef. The tonnage and quality that could have been added to each animal by feeding was lost.

Controls remained, however, along with rationing and shortage. As in all wartime efforts, mistakes were made, but range production was stepped up prodigiously.

When ration books were put away as souvenirs and the OPA died, Americans were beef hungry, and they had the money to pay the butcher at the corner grocery and the supermarket.

Although the Office of Price Stabilization ceilings at the retail level remained for a time, the price of live cattle slanted sharply upward. Before the cowmen could realize what was taking place, they had a boom on their hands—a rising market which made it possible for a man to buy a dogie in the morning and sell it in the afternoon for enough profit to pay for his dinner and perhaps a few drinks.

It was as perfect a boom as any herd-singing puncher could have dreamed up on a moonlit night on the prairie.

Except for a few spotted dry spells and one winter's White Ruin in the mountain regions (and its damage was cut substantially by the dropping of feed from airplanes in a hay-lift operation), the weather was fine for range production; again in the cow country the windows of Heaven had opened.

But troubles are never far from the cowman's range. In these fine times, one danger signal rose and fluttered high in the Southern sky. An epidemic of foot-and-mouth disease broke out in Mexico not far below Texas. In their battle against the Argentina Sanitary Pact the older rangemen had learned that such a plague could quickly spread to the United States and destroy the beef and dairy industries.

This danger was close to home now, and the Texas and Southwestern was in the first line of battle. C. E. Weymouth, who for years had run parts of the large ranch his father-in-law, the late R. B. Masterson, had started, was then president of the Association. He called his executive committee into emergency session to map plans to stamp out disease in another nation. From this start, the ranchers of the West cooperated with each other once more in their American National.

A joint United States-Mexico commission handled the bout with the disease. Weymouth served on the commission. The presidents who followed him—Bryant Edwards, whose father was a pioneer in the old northwest Texas district, and Ray Willoughby of San Angelo, a leader in all branches of the livestock business—spent nearly all their time in Washington or in Mexico in the campaign to eradicate this danger.

The work—the killing of thousands of cattle and the vaccination of millions—took five years (and the area and the border are still under strict watch late in 1954), but it was doubly successful; the epidemic was stopped and effective methods of controlling the disease were developed.

Men like Weymouth, Edwards and Willoughby knew well the axiom of their forebears that troubles come in herds. They raised their voices against government controls and overproduction. But such advice is seldom heeded in times of rich promise.

There must be bone-deep in all the sons of Adam a desire to own a place in the country with cattle and maybe a horse to ride after the sleek and increasing herd. The opportunity for the great mass of men to realize this desire has come only in boom times, when a man could make enough money to buy in. And, as in the booms of other years, nearly everybody tried to get into the beef cattle business this time. Barbers, utility company workers, doctors, lawyers, merchants, chiefs of police, oil men, cowboys dived right in. Many borrowed money for their plunge. Some of them bought their land; others leased their range. Nearly every piece of real estate looked good for cow pasture.

In timbered eastern Texas and in the Southeastern states all the way to the southern point of Florida old farms were restored to grass and put to cattle. So were submarginal and marsh areas. Florida loomed up as one of the major producers of beef cattle. A good many Midwestern feeders who, as corn farmers, had in the past bought their cattle from range men started raising their own.

The cow country had its greatest expansion.

It was then, at the height of the boom, that a group of New Yorkers, seeing and feeling this wave of range prosperity, decided that the Matador would be an excellent investment. Because of world upheaval and certain tax laws in the British Isles, the Scottish owners of the Matador, who had reaped rich reward for generations from this Texas empire, saw that they could realize more money by selling the ranch than by continuing its profitable operation. They sold.

The new owners then divided the old spread into several land and cattle companies and put it all on the market. Many men in the cattle business wanted a hunk of the Matador. In some cases, veteran cowmen bought parts of it; in other cases, newcomers took on good-sized pieces of it and also bought Matador cows. But the ranch had been an enormous thing, and all of it had not been sold in 1954. The residue was being operated by the group who had bought it from the canny Scots.

In seventy-odd years of boom, bust and change, the Matador had come full circle: born of a boom in which men longed for land and cattle, it was broken up in the same kind of boom.

In this era of frenzied activity on the range, when beef cattle numbers rose to a record and the price of a prime beef animal soared to an all-time high, the Association's detective system remained the same and on the same old job, but with a fantastic new type of sleuthing to do. The up-to-date rustler changed his methods. To a great extent, rustling shifted from the dark prairies to the lighted boulevards. There developed the amazing art of rustling only half a beef.

One day a mystified cowman from Mesquite, which is located almost within the evening shadows of the spires of Dallas, called on Association Manager Henry Bell. That morning the cowman had found, not far from a busy highway, a dead cow; her hindquarters had been slashed off and were gone; the cut had been made just back of the brand on the $300 cow's side. There were man and car tracks, indicating the facts of the story: men in a car had pulled off the pavement, quickly knocked the cow in the head, slashed off the unbranded hindquarters, stowed their beef in the trunk of the car, and were gone, no doubt to a home deepfreeze.

At about the same time, Inspector John E. Hodges was called on a similar case just outside San Antonio; the animal slashed and killed was a young registered Hereford bull worth $1,300. Many a rancher, and even dairymen, all over the cow country lost unbranded calves; the beef rustler could knock down a calf and stuff it whole into the trunk of a car.

This sort of rustling may have been a result of high living costs and the uncertainties of the times. Teeming thousands of people were crowded into the vicinities of defense plants and growing industrial areas—living in housing projects and trailer camps. They paid high prices at the store for their beef. On drives in the country and along highways they could see the sleek Herefords or black Angus grazing on the green grass or chewing cuds contentedly in the shade of a grove. Such a scene could generate temptation—for food or for money.

Yet cattle rustling remained a major crime as well. A once prosperous businessman in the Fort Worth-Dallas area over-expanded and failed. In a desperate attempt to recoup, he went out at night, stole cattle and trucked them to San Antonio. The inspectors were soon on his trail, and when he saw them coming he eased the muzzle of a loaded shotgun into his mouth and pulled the trigger.

A Houston lady on her way home from the grocery store happened to glance through a crack in the door of a resi-dential garage, and she thought she saw a man skinning a cow. Being conscious of the beef situation and the fact that cattle rustling was in the news, she hurried home and tele-phoned the police station.

The police notified Association Inspector G. O. Stoner, who for forty-odd years had chased rustlers and had sent at least a thousand of them to prison. He turned up at the garage and caught a new kind of rustler red-handed. There was the carcass; also the hide bearing the brand of an Association member. With this start, Stoner developed the case against two city men who had stolen forty-eight cattle and had peddled the beef to eating places, small retail markets and unfastidious, meat-hungry individuals.

Then within a few days Stoner shifted from the very new to the very old in rustling. Answering a hurry-up call to a ranch near Houston, he found two neighbors at each other's throat—arguing hotly over sixteen cattle that each claimed. Stoner ended the embryonic feud by finding that both men were right. A quick examination by the sharp-eyed inspector revealed that modern rustlers had worked the old, old trick of brand-burning. Back-tracking the trail of the beeves, Stoner discovered that rustlers had stolen them from one of the neighbors and hauled them to another county. There the rustlers had changed the brand. After the running-iron burn had healed, the cattle were taken to San Antonio and sold. The buyer took them to a nearby auction and resold them. The buyer this time was the second neighbor; he hauled the cattle home and put them in his pasture across the fence from where they had nibbled grass before they were stolen. Stoner's ability to go back over this trail proved disastrous for the rustlers.

One of the most wanton cases of rustling hit the Furd Halsell ranch in northern Texas. One spring about two hundred cows were found dead on the rolling range and there were no bawling orphaned calves around. Each cow had been killed by a blow on the head.

When inspectors started delving for clues they checked the Fort Worth cattle market. Several loads of unbranded calves had been sold there at about the time the cows were killed. It would do no good in solving the case to find the calves and return them to the range, for there would be no waiting mothers to claim them and thereby establish legal evidence; that was the reason the cows had been killed by the thieves, who were wise to the ways of the range. Nonetheless, the men who had sold the calves were good suspects. Keen-eyed Bill Luman went over the range, yard by yard. He studied all horse and man tracks, and had casts made of several of them. Then he made casts of the hoofs of the horses belonging to the suspects. Certain matching nicks showed up in the casts of the tracks and the hoofs. This bit of modern sleuthing sent three men to prison, and the wholesale mother-cow killing ceased on that range.

But the inspectors, expert as they are, don't catch all the thieves. In almost every case they are called in days or weeks after cattle are stolen, for a rancher may not miss cattle until then. So it is that the inspector usually starts on a cold trail. But some modern thieves leave plain tracks. On the big

JA Ranch in the Texas Panhandle (the original Goodnight-Adair spread), an old cow with a milking-time look bellowed around, and there was no calf. Inspector Alan Jefferies was called in to take a look. There on the range were the tracks of a pickup truck. They zigzagged, twisted, turned, leaving in their wake a swath of flattened and peeled mesquite. Finally, there were the tracks of a calf where, in being reluctantly dragged, it had plowed its four little feet into the ground. Since there were no human or horse tracks, Jefferies visualized this one as a really modern method. It was clear that one man had driven the truck, dodging after the calf like a roping horse, and another man had stood in the back of the truck twirling his lasso and dropping the loop expertly over the calf's neck.

This case still mystifies Inspector Jefferies, and he hasn't quit looking for the dexterous driver of that pickup that pinch-hit for a horse.

To outwit an Association inspector is an infrequent achievement worth crowing about, but there are rustlers who can boast of such feats. Inspector Jefferies was stopped one day at a cattle sale by an old man with a devilish glint in his eyes.

"Jefferies," he said, "you can quit watching me now. I've been stealing cattle for years, and you've never quite got the goods on me. Now I'm quitting. Getting too old. I'm retiring."

The thief quit at about the right time. Not long after this conversation a newspaper story told of a man who had stolen several cattle and a week or so later had attempted to return them to the rightful owner. The owner refused to take them back, saying, "Oh, no. You stole them; now you find grass and spend money buying feed for them."

Western cowmen of all generations have voiced the opinion that since the time of Noah there has never yet been quite enough rain to suit them. That old bugaboo, drought, starts creeping at first and then gets a good hold while men hope for rain; and suddenly one day the range is the dead-yellow color of sun-burnt grass and the waterholes are dry, the earthen bottoms cracked open into thousands of miniature crumbly crevices.

In the late 1940's from the brushy plateaus along the unhurried Rio Grande, where the Texas cattle business began with the tough old longhorns a century or more ago, drought burned northward in a wide swath; eventually it followed the pattern of the dust bowl of the 1930's, extending into Kansas and parts of Oklahoma, Louisiana, Arkansas, Missouri, New Mexico and Colorado and edging into the beautiful green hills of Wyoming. In springtime high winds swept this vulnerable arid country relentlessly, and the sky filled with dust.

Stunned ranchers tried to find reasons for the visitation. From one end of the dry country to the other, there were folks who wondered whether the atomic bomb had "messed up" the weather. One man said he had it straight that soon after the first atomic blast went off in New Mexico, the cows for miles around turned a grizzled white. If man's tinkering with the atom could do that to cows, he reasoned, it could banish clouds.

In the parched country near Uvalde, where Dolph Briscoe and John N. Garner still dwelt, word-of-mouth reports spread a rumor that the Navy, which had a practice range for planes nearby and needed fair skies for flying, had developed a magic medicine with which it dissolved every cloud that ventured into the brassy sky in that vicinity.

Frantic reports of this, many of them by seasoned cowmen, poured into the Texas and Southwestern offices in Fort Worth—with demands that something be done. Association Manager Bell relayed this information to Joe Montague, who was in Washington, with instructions to get the facts. Montague went into a huddle with R. B. Anderson, then Secretary of the Navy. Anderson could understand the ranchers' desire to investigate even remote reasons for the devastation of drought. He had long managed the vast Waggoner estate of land, cattle and oil and had served on the directorate of the Texas and Southwestern until his appointment to the Eisenhower Cabinet. He called in naval officers and laid the rumors before them. The latter knew of no such operation, and the Texas and Southwestern put out a special bulletin which relieved the Navy of the responsibility for sustaining the drought.

By the spring of 1952, heavy selling of cattle off drought-stricken range had cracked the market and sent prices shooting downward in a record slump. Frenzied selling by newcomers, who wanted to get out while the getting was good, kept flooding the market and forcing it downward. Almost before they knew what was happening many men awakened to the fact that they were ruined; cows for which they had paid up to $300 each would, even with frisky calves at their sides, do well to bring $100. The only way to keep them alive was to buy feed, for there was no grass. The cow country was full of men who owed more on their cattle, and for feed, than their herds would bring. Some of the men who had bought Matador land and cattle wished they had stayed out.

One Kansas man, a former automobile dealer, had plunged into cattle raising and financing in a big way in Kansas, Oklahoma and Texas. "When the bust came," he said, "if I had

had all my money in coins and in a granary I couldn't have scooped it out as fast as I lost it."

Many veteran cowmen, and also some bankers, were likewise caught; they had overexpanded and overextended credit. Aglow with the enthusiasm generated by prosperity, they had forgotten the gospel of the cow business that, ever since Joseph sent food out of Egypt to his hungry brethren in a drought-stricken land, the cattle business had been a thing of good and lean years. They might well have remembered the words spoken in the lean year of 1921 by W. W. Turney, president of the Association in 1903-06 and again when Texas Cattle Raisers became the Texas and Southwestern:

Speaking as a banker, as well as a cattleman, let me tell you that you are only safe when you have such investment in your own business as that no other institution's or man's loans to you can destroy you, and when you have reached that situation, you can battle against drought; you can battle against these money panics; you can say, regardless of these failures that come, they cannot, like they did in 1920 and 1921, take and destroy the accumulations of a life-time.

It was more natural in 1953 than in "the good old days" to look to Washington. One thing that made this bust the worst of all was the high price of cow feed, which was caused by the federal government's long-time farm price support program. Under this, the government guaranteed minimum prices on a good many products, such as cotton and grain, and these prices made cow feed come dear for the man with no grass.

Midwestern corn farmers who usually buy range cattle and feed them found the price of beef could go down faster than the animals could put on pounds; in some cases the feeders didn't make as much by feeding as they could simply by selling their corn to the government at support prices. This narrowed the demand for beef cattle.

Beef cattle producers had not been standing on this government-guaranteed price floor. But in the violently hot summer of 1953, a good many newcomers who had lost their shirts, as well as some bankers and old-timers, petitioned Washington for help and demanded support prices for beef cattle.

This was somewhat startling news to President Eisenhower, the first man of the cattlelands to be chief executive since Teddy Roosevelt, having been born, as he said, on one end of the Chisholm Trail and having grown up on the other end of the famed cattle highway. He was born in Denison, Texas, in old Northwest Texas Stock Raisers territory, in 1890, at about the time A. P. Bush and other veterans started making suggestions to the railroads, packers and the federal government. He grew up in Abilene, Kansas, the first terminus of the Old Chisholm.

Between the time of General Eisenhower's election and inaugural, cowmen, led by the Texas and Southwestern, petitioned him to remove all controls and turn the cattle business loose. They conferred with him in Denver and told him they wanted no government subsidies. New Mexico Ranchman Albert Mitchell was credited with the remark that expressed the spirit of most of the cow country: "We want no government control. If trouble comes we prefer to hump up and take it."

Claiming they "had been taken as the Indians took Custer," the others who demanded price supports kept up their fight.

But the cowmen—the Texas and Southwestern, the American National and every major organization of beef stockmen in the range states—stood pat, claiming that a support program would be impossible to administer, that it would raise the price of beef to the consumer and that it would mean government running of the cow business.

Jack Roach, who had learned to ride a horse and chase after cows as a Texas farm boy and had grown big in ranching without oil wells or government aid, was president of the Texas and Southwestern. He summed up the majority attitude of the old outfit:

. . . We feel that any price support program would necessarily carry with it production controls and the very nature of the cattle business makes such controls unfeasible and impractical, as well as distasteful to every experienced cattle producer.

The cowmen reiterated this stand at their 1954 annual meeting in March. At this session, Roy Parks of Midland was elected president of the Texas and Southwestern. He had learned ranching in the old Northwest Texas Raisers territory, riding with the newer generations of Lynches, Matthews and Reynolds. In 1918, he had moved to far western Texas where there was more room for a man to spread out. Parks took up the fight against government controls.

In "humping up and taking it," the cowmen launched a program on their own, a healthy plan designed to encourage American appetites to take care of any beef surplus, and also to permit increased production. Joined by the packers, other processors and major retail outlets, they started an "eat more beef" advertising campaign, its goal to double the consumption of beef within ten years.

To a great extent, this is the gospel of the cow business as preached by C. C. Slaughter, back in Baltimore years ago when he was there attending a Baptist convention.

In 1954, Jay Taylor found himself back in the beef advertising arena. He was elected president of the American National, the organization which, with the help of the National Live Stock and Meat Board in Chicago, was chosen to handle this beef-eating campaign. In that summer, big "Eat More Beef" signs went up on billboards, with smaller ones gracing the windshields and rear windows of automobiles.

Taylor promptly announced that the old solitary, "shrink back into the shell" attitude had to go, that cowmen must promote public relations and replace "Keep Out" signs on their ranches with "Welcome" mats at their doors and a display of their brands along highways and roads; this to be done so that touring Americans could grow more familiar with ranches and the way in which the steaks they liked for dinner were produced.

Late in that year, with rain spattering at the drought in scattered areas and without help from the government except a program of emergency feed, some surplus beef buying and an easing of credit, the cattle business had regained stability and was starting its uphill climb. At least, it had improved to the point where the rustler was busy again. Perhaps the rustler—much to his personal detriment—in addition to being the instigator has done more than anything else to keep the cowmen working together alertly and progressively the past eighty years—an evil agent that brought together forces of integrity and honor.

In 1954, two Texas and Southwestern inspectors in Oklahoma, Pete Howell of Marlow and Coy Rosenthal of Antlers, broke up a rustling gang that had rounded up and made off with some two hundred cattle near Ada, Oklahoma. These rustlers had grown ingenious and by employing a new device they came very close to solving the thorny problem of getting rid of telltale branded cowhides. They encased the hides in old automobile tires and then blithely burned the tires. The odor of the burning rubber concealed that of the hides.

This worked for a while, but the range detectives surprised them one perfumed February morning, and these latter-day rustlers joined the ranks of renegades for whom the Association inspectors had made this supreme crime of the West a thing of no profit at all.

Out West under spacious skies the land still seems to stretch from sea to shining sea, and the long-reaching barbed-wire fences blend into the rough countryside even at a short distance away. The freedom of life in the cattlelands—and the day-to-day struggle for its preservation—is still a reality for men who want space to breathe in.

The State of Texas has placed a marble marker in the shade of the cowmen's tree in the City of Graham close to its neatly paved main street, thus designating an historic spot. The tree has weathered many a drought and blizzard. It has lost some branches but it has gained in height and taken on a few gnarls, giving it a look of rough invincibility. It stands there still, the original milepost on the long, long trail of Texas and Southwestern cowmen.

Acknowledgments

The basic sources of information for this book have been the records of the Texas and Southwestern Cattle Raisers Association and its monthly magazine, *The Cattleman*. From the first meeting of these cowmen to the most recent one, detailed minutes have been kept. These minutes—written in a scrawling hand for a good many years—reflect conditions, past and present, in the beef cattle business throughout the cow country. As far as was humanly possible, every event related in this book was checked against the records of the Association.

The Cattleman was not established until 1914, far too late for the early days when printed records and even good newspaper reports were scarce. However, many an old-timer in mellowing years unreeled his memory and turned out stories for the magazine. Moreover, almost numberless cowmen, cowboys and range detectives were interviewed by writers and their stories published in *The Cattleman*. In this way, virtually the entire story of the cattle industry in the Southwest has been recorded in the magazine. The big job was that of searching out the facts and anecdotes and collecting them in this narrative.

Quite a few notable writers of the Southwest cut their teeth on *The Cattleman*. Some of the first writing of J. Frank Dobie, the leading historian and folklorist of the region, appeared in the magazine. In this way, Mr. Dobie, by personal knowledge and by deft research, preserved for reference some excellent material.

So did Everett Edward Dale, a leading historian of Oklahoma, who was for a long time a range-riding cowboy. His articles in *The Cattleman* told in engaging detail the story of Texas cowmen and the Indian lands.

Mary Whatley Clarke has written for the magazine a biographical sketch of each Association president, and she has contributed many other articles of historical value. These were very helpful in the work of piecing together this narrative.

Floyd Benjamin Streeter did an exhaustive job of research on the National Cattle Trail, and his article on the subject was also published in the magazine.

The line drawings are by Harold Bugbee of Clarendon, Texas, one of the best known of Western artists. These drawings were made available to me by Henry Biederman, editor of *The Cattleman*, and I am grateful to both him and Mr. Bugbee for permission to reproduce them here.

Mr. Biederman also suggested the use of the full-color painting, "The Roundup" by Charles M. Russell, from the Malcolm S. Mackay collection of Russell paintings. I deeply appreciate the kindness of the Historical Society of Montana in making possible its reproduction in this volume.

Henry Bell, long-time secretary-manager of the Association, spent many hours in helping track down information and otherwise aiding in this work.

Three cowmen whose families have been in the Association since its start—Joe B. Matthews, Watt Matthews and Joe Reynolds—went patiently over the entire manuscript. So did Mary Whatley Clarke (the unofficial historian of the Association) and Editor Biederman. These first readers made numerous helpful suggestions.

Others who have been especially helpful in various ways include the present Association president, Roy Parks; Ray Willoughby, Chanslor Weymouth, Jay Taylor, Jack Roach, Claude McCan and Bryant Edwards, all former presidents; Attorney Joe Montague (who prosecutes the rustlers); and Inspectors Charles A. Stewart, J. E. Hodges, A. T. Jefferies, J. W. Luman, G. O. Stoner and N. H. Sweeney.

The research goes further back. In the mid-1930's I began reporting livestock activities for the daily press of Texas. This work took me often to see Berkley Spiller, long-time secretary of the Association and grandson of Jim Loving. He related a good many stories of the early days as passed down in his family. It was mainly through these interviews that the story of the first years of the frontier cowmen was pieced together.

The author had the good fortune to "chin" with many old-timers, such as Trail-driver Ab Blocker, before they passed on, and a part of this story came firsthand from the tales they told.

My parents, Mr. and Mrs. C. T. Nordyke, and my wife's parents, Mr. and Mrs. R. I. Beeman, are of people who have been in the West since the beginning of the beef cattle business. Therefore, I grew up with, and still live with, stories of the rangelands.

Undoubtedly three of the very best reference works on the Southwestern and Western beef cattle industry are *The Cattle Industry of Texas and Adjacent Territory, 1895*, edited by James Cox and privately published; *The Trail Drivers of Texas*, compiled and edited by J. Marvin Hunter and published under the direction of George W. Saunders; and *Historic Sketches of the Cattle Trade of the West and*

Southwest by Joseph G. McCoy, the man who made Abilene. This latter book was published in 1874 by Ramsey, Millett and Hudson, Kansas City, Missouri.

I have made this full statement on sources and reference material so that the use of footnotes could be avoided in the text of this story.

My special thanks to John C. Willey of William Morrow & Co. of New York City. He has been the guiding light of this work from the start. He is an understanding editor.—L. N.

Index